Intricate Passions

Edited by Tee Corinne

BANNED BOOKS
Austin, Texas

Contents

A very special thank you to both Carol Seajay and Lee Lynch who helped me dream this book into existence, and to Beverly Brown for her assistance in the manuscript's final, exciting hours.

Introduction

In the introductions to my books of erotica writing: *Lovers* and *Dreams of the Woman Who Loved Sex*, I wrote of my search for sexually explicit reading material, and the herstory of lesbian-produced stories and poems. While writing those introductions, I began to envision a collection of contemporary stories which would reflect, in varying ways, the inclusiveness of the second wave of the Women's Movement.

I contacted 36 lesbian writers, most of whom were widely published in the feminist press, asking them to contribute stories that "focus on the sexual, that reveal character through sexuality, and that celebrate physical and emotional loving."

Twenty-four women responded with the stories you will find in this book. I contributed the twenty-fifth. Stylistically the stories vary from the edge of poetry to the detailed documentary. Psychologically they roam the non-violent gamut.

The youngest author is Kathrine Davis, twenty-five, a rape crisis counselor, and the most senior is veteran novelist Valeric Taylor, seventy-six, a Gay Gray Panther and peace activist.

Although most of the stories were written specifically for this anthology, I've included some which have appeared elsewhere. "All We really Are Is Open" was published in "Country Woman Magazine" in 1975 and seems to me as fresh and daring today as it did when I first read it.

Contributors' photographs are included to remind all of us that real women write these stories, women with identities and experiences far greater than can be contained in any single story or group of stories. Biographical notes and personal statements appear at the end of the book as a way to share more of who we are, where we've come from, why we choose to write about sexuality.

This anthology is grounded in the place and time in which it was produced. It could only come into existence now, after almost twenty years of work by lesbian presses; after thirty-three years of lesbian magazine publication: periodicals which gave many of these writer their first exposure, so to speak.

Enjoy.

Tee A. Corinne
June 28, 1989

La Maya

Terri de la Peña

Adriana Carranza tossed off her beach robe, and the morning sun kissed her glistening skin. She flexed her brown toes along the white Caribbean sand and walked into the waves. They met her lazily and Adriana fell into their billowing embrace. She swam with assurance and laughed when curious yellow fish darted between her legs. Their fluttering fins reminded her of Liz's flirting tongue.

After an invigorating swim, Adriana closed her eyes and floated. This was her last day on Isla Mujeres. Tomorrow she would travel to the Yucatan peninsula to Chichen Itza and Tulum. Liz had wanted to come on this trip, but Adriana had refused her company. Years ago, she had traveled to Mexico with Marisol, but they had by-passed Yucatan. Adriana had always regretted not seeing the Mayan pyramids. This time around, she did not want to view them with an Anglo lover. And so she had come alone.

While she floated, Adriana mused about what had brought Liz and her together. Both bilingual teachers, they had met at a weekend conference. Adriana had been single then, and found herself susceptible to Liz's rapid pursuit. But once their sexual obsession had faded, they existed on different wavelengths. Liz had gone into bilingual instruction for the extra pay, not from any genuine love of the language and culture of Latinas. Increasingly, Adriana had sensed this, and had planned this vacation without her.

The caressing water licked her sensuously. Adriana had noticed that the tropical climate heightened her sexuality. For several nights, she had had erotic dreams, not about Liz, but about brown-skinned Mexicanas with glossy hair and compelling eyes. She wondered if being among her own people had made her more open to these fantasies.

She noticed she had floated away from the shoreline. Alone in the water, she touched herself fleetingly. Her skin tingled at the slight pressure of her fingertips. Adriana slowly moved her hand lower, her long fingers grazing below her bikini's borders. Her tuft was thick and damp.

Turquoise water intermingled with her own moistness. She sighed and slipped her middle finger within.

Closing her eyes, she imagined herself lying in shallow water with a naked Mayan woman beside her. La Maya's body seemed sturdy and powerful. Long ebony hair cascading into her face, she did not speak. Her onyx-black eyes studied Adriana, as if challenging her, before she gently unsnapped the bikini. At Adriana's barely perceptible nod, la Maya's skillful fingers began to pleasure her. She bent over the reclining woman, and her budding nipples peaked at brushing against Adriana's welcoming thighs. Her brown fingers teased Adriana relentlessly, and she moaned, her outstretched legs wrapping themselves around la Maya's wide hips.

La Maya smiled at Adriana's impulsiveness, and she leaned over her, white teeth gleaming, broad lips anticipating the womanly feast. Her skin exuded a musky scent, and her nimble tongue licked Adriana repeatedly. Adriana wanted to blend with esta mujer extraña, and she grabbed the thick ends of la Maya's flowing hair. Her cabello de india felt like a lifeline. Adriana clung to her while la Maya's tongue provoked, her teeth nibbled, and her fingers fondled.

Adriana's pleasure was so intense she did not care if she drowned. Her head lay propped against flat stones and she felt herself sink as la Maya feasted upon her. Her warm lips surrounded Adriana's clitoris possessively, and her fingers wandered inside her. Adriana gasped, and the still water rippled when she came, urgently, strongly.

When she opened her eyes and found herself alone, Adriana knew she had been dreaming, but she felt relaxed, fulfilled. The sudden afternoon rain drizzled upon her floating body, bouncing off her, recalling the intimate feel of la Maya's adoring tongue. Adriana wondered if such a woman existed — and if so — where would she find her?

☆ ☆ ☆

She leaned against the registration counter in the lobby of El Hotel Chichen Itza. Already a few other tourists had gathered, awaiting their guide to the Mayan archaeological sites. Because of the humidity, Adriana had moussed her short black hair and brushed it away from her brow. The sleek style emphasized her tawny skin and candid brown eyes. Her small-boned figure looked sporty in a short-sleeved shirt, safari shorts and huaraches. She had risen early to swim, wondering if la Maya would come to her again. She had not.

Adriana felt edgy. She toyed with the Nikon hanging around her neck and was eager to start the tour. Except for situations like this, she enjoyed traveling alone. Otherwise, she was awkward with small talk, and stood apart from the rest of the tourists. Adriana had already rebuffed the interest of a lean German. Didn't any other dykes travel this far south? So far, she had not seen any. She wondered if she would.

Next to the registration desk, she revolved the postcard rack, trying to decide whether to drop Liz a line. Funny how she had hardly thought about her this trip. Being with these other Americans — many had already asked if she were a Mexican citizen — reminded her of the contrasts between Liz and her. Liz was a tall and lean Coloradan, with curly blond hair and sparkling green eyes. She played on a softball team and liked country-western music, while California-born Adriana preferred reading lesbian novels and listening to salsa. Opposites attract, she reminded herself, but they can also become boring.

From the corner of her eye, Adriana noticed her. La mujer glided into the lobby with the grace of a prowling jaguar. She was lithe and brown, of average height — but there was nothing average about her. Her waist-length black hair was fastened with a golden clasp at the nape of her neck. Her penetrating eyes spoke of ageless mysteries. With a Mayan profile, she seemed to have stepped from the pages of a Mexican art book. She had the prominent nose, the sensual lips, the large eyes with the slight upward tilt so characteristic of the Mayans. She even wore an embroidered huipil, a short version which revealed her strong legs. Adriana stared. La Maya had come to life.

La mujer halted before the assembled tourists. "Bienvenidos a Chichen Itza. I am Pilar de Oro, your guide." Her Spanish-tinged accent charmed the tourists. Adriana braced herself against the registration counter. Her knees had gone weak.

⚹ ⚹ ⚹

Into Chichen Itza, the seat of Mayan-Toltec culture, Pilar led the tourists. She explained how in 1000 A.D. the Itza people, a branch of the Toltecs, had conquered Mayan territory and gained control over Yucatan and parts of Guatemala. In her husky voice, she pointed out the nine-staged El Castillo, built over a smaller pyramid, and promised to take them inside later.

Adriana hardly listened to Pilar's narrative. She was too intrigued with watching her, anticipating how to approach her. Liz and their problems vanished from Adriana's thoughts. Pilar proved a fitting distraction.

Near the Well of Sacrifice, a rock-walled cistern where Mayan virgins had been offered to the gods, Adriana stepped closer to the guide.

"You'd think the spirits of those virgins would haunt this place." She glanced at Pilar with the trace of a smile.

Pilar's ebony eyes met hers. "Sometimes they cry out at night."

Adriana like the way Pilar's eyebrows moved expressively; otherwise she wore an impassive Mayan mask. Adriana sensed the guide offered a local legend. "Estás jugando, verdad?"

"No sabía que hablabas español." Pilar gazed at her intently. "Muchas norteamericanas no les gusta hablar nuestro idioma."

Hearing her speak Spanish, Adriana melted. She longed to unfasten the golden clasp and set Pilar's lengthy hair free. She wanted to wrap herself in it, but she restrained herself and tried to focus on their conversation.

"Pues, soy Chicana. Me encanta hablar español." She pushed aside a stray strand of her own hair. "Have you really heard the voices de las Mayas?"

"Of course," Pilar insisted. Her voice became secretive. "They moan and wail durante la noche. Some say it is the wind, but I know it is the virgins."

Pilar was really giving her the tour guide spiel, Adriana thought. She grinned, aimed the camera at the cistern and snapped a couple of shots. When she had finished, she let the camera dangle again. "How pathetic that those women died without knowing love."

As Pilar tossed her long hair over her shoulder, it fell against a round breast. Adriana wanted to smooth those dark strands over Pilar's womanly contours. The guide's face betrayed the hint of a smile. "Ah, but the virgins considered it an honor to be sacrificed."

"Then why do they cry at night?"

"If you hear them, you will know."

☆ ☆ ☆

After they had explored the great Ball Court, the Temple of the Warriors and The Court of the Thousand Columns, Pilar led her turistas across the site to El Caracol, the ruins of the astronomical observatory. While the tourists examined the apertures in the ruins' exterior walls, Pilar explained how the Mayans had formulated their calendar. Adriana leaned quietly against one wall and waited for another chance to speak with Pilar. Soon the turistas spread out with their cameras, and Adriana followed her down the steps of El Caracol.

"Pilar—"

The guide turned and nodded when Adriana caught up with her. "Sí?"

"Talk with me."

Pilar gestured towards Adriana's camera. "No more film?"

Adriana smiled. "Let me take a picture of you. Por favor, eh?"

With some reluctance, Pilar positioned herself at the foot of the steps and did not move until Adriana had photographed her. She looked solemn, but provocative.

"Grácias, Pilar." Adriana walked along with her. "How long have you been conducting these tours?"

"Muchos años. I cherish the history of my people."

"It's amazing how much you actually resemble the Mayan carvings and murals," Adriana blurted out. She mentally kicked herself. It had been a while since she had flirted so openly.

"It helped in getting this job," Pilar admitted with a short laugh. "What about you? De donde viene su familia?"

"Vera Cruz. My grandparents were born there." Adriana wished she could spend the whole afternoon learning to know ésta mujer. "Are you from Chichen Itza?"

"Nací en un pueblito cerca de aqui." Pilar sat on one of the rough steps. "What brought you here?

Adriana shrugged. "Curiosity, mostly. I've always wanted to see all this. I plan to show these slides to my students."

"Ah, you're a teacher."

"Yes. Elementary school. Chicano kids need to be aware of their history." Adriana stepped back a few feet and took a long shot of El Caracol. "Pilar, have you ever been to the United States?"

The guide shook her dark head. "I belong here."

Before Adriana could respond, Pilar moved away to round up the tourists.

☆ ☆ ☆

Adriana switched off the light and stood for a moment at the window of her hotel room. The full moon shone luminescently, reflected in the deserted swimming pool. It seemed like a giant pearl suspended in the obsidian sky.

Slipping into bed, Adriana nestled against the pillow and thought about the Chichen Itza tour. The tourists had straggled behind Pilar into El Castillo, laboriously climbing its narrow steps to view the Throne of the Red Jaguar at the summit. Adriana remembered the slimy feel of the pyramid's humid walls, and how expertly Pilar had risen to the top of the steep staircase. She had tiny feet and moved nimbly, her voice echoing within the stifling enclosure. Adriana had found the interior claustrophobic, and had hurried out. After that, she had been unable to engage Pilar in further conversation.

She wondered if Pilar had avoided her. Had she sensed Adriana's attraction to her? Or was she simply keeping a professional distance from tourists? Adriana could not be certain.

She glanced at her watch and decided to read. Picking up her novel, she pored over its intricate plot. And then she heard the sound — an eerie wail, followed by a shuddering sigh, an uneasy silence. Adriana put down her book and lay still. She heard the piercing sound again. She shivered, recalling long ago tales of La Llorona, the weeping woman who lured disobedient children to their deaths. But no, this unearthly sound could only be the wind howling through the trees.

Discomfited, Adriana rose and paused by the window once more. She saw nothing, only the suspended moon, the empty pool. She stared into the inky night for several moments. When she was about to return to bed, she spied a shadowy movement at the far end of the pool. Someone glided beyond the hotel grounds in the direction of the pyramids. Adriana strained to make out the form. She caught a glimpse of flying black hair and a diaphanous white huipil. And then that throaty voice called to her.

"Adriana — Adriana. Ven conmigo ésta noche."

She remained immobile. Heart thudding, Adriana thought she recognized the voice. Listening to it again, she knew she had to find out. Reaching for her seersucker robe, she slipped it on and opened the window.

☆　☆　☆

In the distance, she viewed the stark outline of El Castillo and the other Mayan structures. Adriana hurried towards them, and then stopped momentarily, wondering which direction to take.

"Adriana — aquí éstoy."

She ran towards the Temple of the Warriors and halted at the foot of its staircase.

"Aquí, Adriana — adelante."

Almost crawling, Adriana advanced up the ancient steps and arrived breathless. At the apex of the temple sat la Maya, a resplendent goddess enthroned upon the sculpture of the Rain God, Chac Mool. Her huipil lay forgotten beside her. La Maya's strong brown legs were spread to reveal her vulva, and her black mane was loose, covering her breasts like a feathery shield. Her onyx eyes summoned Adriana.

She stumbled closer and knelt at her feet. La Maya's right hand gently lifted Adriana's yearning face. She leaned forward and her fragrant breath tantalized Adriana. La Maya beckoned her nearer and kissed her, her broad lips covering Adriana's, her passionate tongue invading her mouth. Adriana shivered with desire. She clasped la Maya's vibrant body to her, luxuriating in the heat of her generous breasts.

But Adriana was not satisfied with only kissing. Eventually, she released herself and found la Maya's dark nipples. Adriana filled her mouth with one, then the other, her hands kneading and caressing la Maya's bountiful breasts. And she drew her scorching lips further along la Maya's magnificent body until she reached the treasure sought.

La Maya leaned back on her primitive throne and opened her legs wider. Adriana crouched before her, hungrily tasting la Maya's musky nectar. La Maya kept her hand on Adriana's head, holding her there. She groaned with each stroke of Adriana's eager tongue and squirmed when she lightly bit her clitoris. Adriana seized it between her lips and sucked it longingly, alternately licking and nibbling it. La Maya could hardly keep from sliding off the throne. At her tumultuous orgasms, she screamed Adriana's name, and her primeval cry reverberated amidst the temple's stone pillars.

Adriana slowly raised her head to find la Maya with her head thrown back, her legs still apart. Adriana could not see la Maya's face, but even in the darkness she sensed a difference. When la Maya straightened her posture and faced the woman who had pleased her, Adriana blinked and looked again.

"She's really you," she whispered.

Pilar tossed her hair and smiled ephemerally. "I came for you, Adriana. And I want you to stay — para siempre."

Adriana squatted before her. Her heart pounded from excitement and fear, and she trembled from her cramped position. She had become stiff and sore from kneeling on the uneven stones. but her longing was urgent. "I don't understand, Pilar."

Pilar's eyes were intense. "Let me love you, and then you will know. Ven conmigo."

She stood in one graceful motion and covered herself with the huipil. Pilar's black hair fell upon her shoulders like a silken mantle. She held out her hand to Adriana.

"A donde?" Adriana rose and held Pilar's hand. It was warm, and very tempting.

"To El Caracol."

Las mujeres began to walk together. Adriana had so many questions, but she could not even put them into words. She wondered if she were bewitched, but she was too captivated by her compañera to care if Pilar were a bruja — or a ghost. All she knew was that she wanted to be possessed by this passionate Mayan. Nothing else mattered.

In El Caracol, Pilar led Adriana to a hemp mat in one corner of the ruin. There were flickering candles beside it.

"When I saw you today—against this wall, I knew I could lure you back."

Adriana looked at her and began to undress.

"You seemed so aloof, Pilar."

"Así es mi modo—por el dia." Pilar pulled the huipil over her head and flung it into a corner. "But at night, necesito el amor de una mujer." She came closer and pressed her fingers to Adriana's lips. "Ahora—no more talk."

Adriana's tongue flicked against Pilar's fingers, and in moments las mujeres kissed torridly. They sank to the hemp mat and lay together, their brown bodies entwined. Pilar nicked the tips of Adriana's nipples with her sharp teeth, and her compañera quivered with pleasure.

In the candlelight, Adriana marvelled at the richness of Pilar's body—so voluptuous, so womanly, so Mexicana. She curled herself against Adriana, her skin like fine velvet. Pilar's black hair streamed over them both, and Adriana cherished its feathery texture against her breasts and arms.

"Ay, Pilar."

And Pilar's lips covered hers again, overwhelming her with their intensity. Their tongues danced together, and their bodies blended lustily. Pilar's mouth was suddenly everywhere, her playful teeth at Adriana's breasts, her searing tongue exploring every crevice. Like a starving jaguar, she lunged upon Adriana's aching clitoris and stimulated it so vigorously that Adriana felt feverish with sexual tension. She nearly exploded with desire and came with savage fervor. Pilar's onyx eyes glittered with satisfaction.

Adriana could hardly speak. She had never known such pleasure, and was still dizzy with rapture. With some effort, she raised herself on one elbow and touched her kneeling lover. "Pilar, por favor—no te vayes."

With an enigmatic smile, Pilar kissed Adriana's hand. She stretched herself beside her compañera and stared into her eyes.

"You will stay?"

Adriana did not hesitate. "Yes."

☆　☆　☆

But at dawn, she found herself alone within El Caracol. There was no trace of Pilar. Feeling bewildered, wondering if she had dreamed the midnight interlude, Adriana sat up groggily. By the mat, she found her nightgown and robe. As she dressed, she noticed faint teeth marks upon her breasts. Adriana smiled. It had not been a dream.

☆　☆　☆

After a swim and breakfast, Adriana wandered into the hotel lobby. At the tour desk, she asked about Pilar and was informed she had left early to guide a tour to Tulum.

Disappointed, Adriana went back to her room and got her camera. She spent the rest of that day photographing El Castillo and its environs. Her actions were automatic; she seemed to be in a trance. She climbed the steps of The Temple of the Warriors and rubbed the worn stone seat of the Chac Mool, as if expecting her Mayan lover to materialize. Every time Adriana remembered their lusty lovemaking, she tingled. After a while, she drifted to El Caracol and peered within its half-intact dome. Last night, its dim interior had been brightened by Pilar's incandescence. Adriana longed for her again. And by late afternoon, she sat in the hotel lobby and tried to read, awaiting Pilar.

☆　☆　☆

Glancing up from her novel, Adriana at last saw Pilar and the tourists stroll in. With her solemn graciousness, Pilar said her farewells and lingered by the tour desk. She seemed to take no notice of Adriana. But from where she sat, Adriana could plainly see the scratches on Pilar's arms and the tiny nicks nearly hidden by her black mane. She smiled to herself and continued to wait.

Soon Pilar padded across the terra cotta floor on her way out.

"Pilar—" Adriana could not stop herself from calling.

She half-turned. "A sús órdenes, Señorita."

Adriana stood beside her and spoke softly. "Sabes que son mís órdenes, Pilar?"

"Los puedo imaginar." Her onyx eyes were amused.

Adriana wanted to hold her then, to never let her go. "I wanted to go to Tulum with you."

Pilar shrugged. "Mañana, eh?"

Adriana marveled at her coolness. It only intensified her desire. "I missed you, Pilar."

Pilar barely touched her shoulder as she passed. "Espérame esta noche."

☆　☆　☆

The opalescent Yucatan moon flooded El Caracol's half dome. In the shadows, Adriana stood waiting, alert eyes searching the deserted ruins for a fleeting glimpse of a white huipil, a mane of black hair. Alone, her senses yearning, Adriana listened for the haunting cry of la Maya.

Glossary of Spanish Words and Phrases

Mexicanas	Mexican women
Ésta mujer extraña	This strange woman
Cabello de india	Indian hair
Huaraches	Sandals
La mujer	The woman
Huipil	Traditional dress
Bienvenidos	Welcome
Estás jugando, verdad?	You're teasing, aren't you?
No sabía que hablabas español	I didn't know you spoke Spanish
Muchas norteamericanas no les gusta hablar nuestro idioma	Some North Americans don't like to speak our language
Pues, soy Chicana	Well, I'm Chicana
Me encanta hablar español	I love to speak Spanish
Durante la noche	During the night
Turistas	Tourists
Por favor	Please
Muchos años	Many years
De donde viene su familia?	Where is your family from?
Nací en un pueblito cerca de aquí	I was born in a little town nearby
La Llorona	The weeping woman (Mexican legend)
Ven conmigo ésta noche	Come with me tonight
Aquí éstoy	I'm here
Adelante	Ahead
Para siempre	Forever
A donde?	Where?
Compañera	Woman companion
Bruja	Witch
Así es mi modo — por el dia	That is my way — by day
Necesito el amor de una mujer	I need the love of a woman
Ahora	Now
Por favor, no te vayes	Please don't go
A sús órdenes	At your service
Sabes que son mís órdenes?	Do you know what my orders are?
Los puedo imaginar	I can imagine them
Espérame esta noche	Wait for me tonight

No Sex

Becky Birtha

If you're reading this story because you think there's going to be some sex in it, forget it. I haven't had any for three years. And I wouldn't write about it if you paid me.

This is a story about a bus trip to Washington for a demonstration — a solid, down-to-earth, serious subject. Shove all your wild fantasies aside. You know as well as I do that nobody can really do anything on a bus anyway.

The buses are leaving from outside the station at six a.m. I'm almost late, as usual. They're all lined up along the boulevard in the charcoal dawn, motors revved up and ready to take off. I don't see anyone from my usual crowd, and I'm lucky to get on a bus at all.

I fling my backpack into the nearest seat while I struggle out of my jacket. My jacket is covered with buttons I've collected from various marches and festivals over the years: "Bread not Bombs." "Contras No, Nicaragua Sí." "Abolish Apartheid — Divest Now." "U.S. Out of North America." "Mother Nature is a Lesbian." "I'm One Too." "For Love and for Life, We're Not Going Back." There's an awkward moment when "God is Coming and is She Pissed!" gets caught on the back pocket of my overalls. The woman in the seat next to mine has to help me get it free. It seems to take her forever.

"Thanks," I mumble when she's finally finished. "O.K. if I sit here?" It's the only empty seat on the bus. I stuff my jacket and my pack up top, while I glance over the rows of seats. Some of the women look vaguely familiar from around the community. But none of my friends are on this bus.

As we pull off past the station and onto the expressway, I start to look around. I don't get much farther than the couple across the aisle from me, and right away I realize I've picked the wrong seat. They're acting like they're in their own private car at a drive-in movie. No — it's more like they're in the movie. And it's rated X. They're almost totally covered up by their jackets that they've spread over them, and a bright green sleeping bag zipped open. But there's a lot of motion

---

11

going on under the jackets and the sleeping bag. And they're not being terribly quiet. I can hear some sort of slurping sounds, and then a muffled bunch of giddy giggles.

There's got to be some better scenery between here and Washington, and I turn toward the window. My eyes meet the eyes of the woman who's sharing my seat, after she finally manages to drag hers away from Venus and Sappho, across the aisle. She grins at me, a conspirator's grin. "Don't you think watching it's almost as good as doing it?" she asks for openers.

I can't imagine that she expects a rational answer to this one, and just stare at her, probably with my mouth open, and my face graduating through several different shades of purple. I search for something else to focus on besides her amusement at my reactions. Not across the aisle. I try for the window again, but get stuck on her face.

It's kind of cute — round and sweet with a snub of a nose, lush, full lips, and an aura of wild, frizzy hair all around the edges. Of her face, I mean. Not her lips. There's a labyris hanging upside down from an ear cuff, and another around her neck. Something about her reminds me of my friend Jerene, who lived in the room next to mine in a collective house, seven years ago. Behind a pair of rectangular, wire-framed glasses, compelling brown eyes are probing mine.

With a shock, I realize she's still waiting for an answer. So I answer. "Not especially."

"No?" She sounds surprised, disappointed. But she plunges right on. "What turns you on?"

"What what?" I gasp. Whatever happened to So what kind of work do you do? Or even What's your name? And is everybody on the bus listening to this ridiculous conversation? It's awfully quiet. I glance nervously around. The lovers have kicked off one pair of sneakers and one pair of leather, pointy-toed boots, and sunk even lower into the depths of the seat. While I watch, a hand reaches out from under the sleeping bag and drops a crumpled sweater onto the floor.

Everyone else on the bus appears to be asleep. After all, it's barely daylight outside.

"A little leather?" she's suggesting. "Rosé and candlelight? Godiva chocolates? Kissing in the rain?"

"Nothing!" I cut her off.

"Nothing?" She's only pretending to be so astonished. Obviously she doesn't believe me. "Maybe I should've asked *who* turns you on. Baby butches? Older femmes? Sophisticated suburban matrons you'd never guess in a million years?"

In spite of myself, my eyes have slipped from her face over the rest of her, trying to guess which of these she considers herself. It's hard to say. In a blue-green jersey and brown corduroys, she's neither butch nor femme, neither old nor young—probably around my age. Of course, she doesn't miss it that I've given her the once over, but it doesn't shut her up. She's getting more specific. "Holly Near? Whoopi Goldberg? Toshi Reagon? I know. Serious politicos who spend all their nights going to meetings, don't care what they look like, and never have time for sex."

"Nobody!" I'm getting louder, but I can't seem to help it. "Nothing! Nothing turns me on."

She's raising her eyebrows, but I plunge on before she can interrupt me. "Just because we're lesbians, everyone assumes we're all supposed to love sex. Everyone assumes we have it all the time. That sex must be the most important activity in our lives. That that's all we think about, and talk about, and read about, and write about, and plan our lives around. Well, I hate sex! I don't care if I never have any again for the rest of my life."

From the seat in back of us, there's a muffled giggle, and I realize I must've woken up more than a few people with this tirade. They might as well hear the rest of my philosophy. "I'll tell you what turns me on. The ERA turns me on! Abortion rights turns me on! Ending violence against women. Lesbians winning custody disputes. Funding for AIDS. Women organizing in Mexico. Feminists talking about issues like ageism and racism and classism. Not women's bodies—women's minds! *That's* what turns me on."

I'm finished. I lunge under the seat for my backpack, and remember that I stuffed it in the overhead rack. So I have to stand up, in full view of my audience, in order to extract an issue of *off our backs* that I brought to read on the bus.

In huge letters across the top of the first two pages I open up to, there's the headline "LESBIANS & SEX." It's an interview with some famous lesbian therapist who wrote a book. I turn the page. There's a feature about S & M practices and safe sex. I pass that up, too. Next is a review of a new book—a collection of erotica. Even in "Dykes to Watch Out For" this month, Mo and Harriet are spending the morning in bed. My most dependable source of radical lesbian-feminist theory has let me down.

I page back the other way, and find a piece titled "For Single Women Only," about how you can begin to explore your identity as a sexual being without getting into a relationship. That one caught my interest.

But my seatmate is reading over my shoulder, watching every move I make. So I pass that by, too, and try to be content reading the latest on the Dalkon Shield.

My companion's finally gotten bored with me; she's falling asleep. Across the aisle, the sleeping bag's heaving up and down and the breathing coming from underneath it is almost as loud as the motor of the bus. I'm not going to watch.

But I can't seem to concentrate on *off our backs*, not even the piece about single women, which I have turned back to once I'm sure my companion is asleep. Instead, I keep thinking about her silly question. It doesn't help that the next paragraph in the article starts out with the same question she asked me: "What turns you on?"

I stare at one of the cast-off sneakers on the floor across the aisle, its worn gray laces still tied in a bow knot.

Knots, I'm thinking, as if that were an intelligent answer. Knots. The way they're tied so tight, the separate strands so enmeshed you can't tell which is which. Something so incredibly graceful in that twisting, winding entanglement. And then, the way they open. How you begin tugging at one of the strings, gently, slowly, fabric rubbing against fabric, rustling, sliding through the loop, coming undone. The way you tug and tug and tug until there's that sudden moment when the whole thing comes unbound and falls apart into two separate pieces in your hands.

This gets so intense that I can't deal with the erotic intensity emanating from just one old sneaker on the floor. I have to shift my gaze.

There's the bright green sleeping bag and the jackets, all heaped together, just gently rising and falling now. Covers, I think. That's it. Heaps of them. Mounds of them. Blankets and afghans and throws. Quilts and comforters and counterpanes. Featherbeds you can sink into, and snuggle down between. Thick padded places. Tumultuous tangles of covers, cozy and snug, and textured and tight. Heavy covers that hug you and hold you and weigh you down, and lie on top of you, and underneath you, and enfold you in their embrace. Layers and layers of them. Or just one — a thin cotton sheet on a steamy summer night, right next to the skin, pulled only halfway up. . . .

It's awfully hot on this bus. The driver ought to turn the heat down. We're on a bridge now, crossing a lake, the sun flashing off the surface of the water. I'd like to dive over the side, right into those cool blue waves. I can't seem to get comfortable. Even my underwear is sticking to me, and I start to wonder if I'm getting my period.

My seatmate is still asleep. Without the angular glasses, her face looks softer, easier, gentler. Her frizzy dark hair is smashed against the white paper napkin that hangs from the seat back. Her mouth is a little open. She's breathing slowly, her breasts rising and falling in the blue-green cotton jersey. There's a row of white buttons down the front of the jersey, from the neck to a point right in the middle between her breasts. The top buttons are open, and the bottom buttons are shut.

Maybe that's the answer. Buttons. I imagine fingering them in the dark, or in the half-light of morning. The way they're smooth under your fingers and flat and round. The way you can run your hand along the row of them and gauge the whole measure of your endeavor. The way you can let it take forever, opening them. The way, sometimes, they're so resistant and tough. Your thumbs pushing them, straining against the edges of the resistant opening. Then there's that moment when something gives, and the resistance is gone, and they slide right through. And the open neck of the shirt is just a notch more open. Then there's the next button.

"Buttons! Two dollars apiece. The money goes toward the funding for the march. I'll be coming around to everybody, so if you want to buy one, have your money ready." It's the bus captain on her official rounds.

The moment's over. My getting up to scrounge for my wallet wakes up my seatmate. She gets up to fish out her money, too. Then it's the bathroom line. To get past, I have to squeeze by a leather clad leg and a bare arm hanging out into the aisle from the seat of our enamored neighbors. I don't look too close. Finally my turn comes. Thank goodness it wasn't my period after all, and I won't have to spend the day in the Port-a-potty lines.

When I get back to the seat, my seatmate's eating a peanut butter sandwich. "Want some?" she asks in a friendly way.

"No thanks." I'm well prepared for lunch. I knew there wasn't going to be anywhere to pick up vegetarian fast food between the Washington Monument and the Capitol, so last night I fried tempeh and made myself a couple of hefty TLTs.

I reach hungrily into the bag and pull out—a stick of butter. A lemon. Three onions.

I have a vague recollection of stopping for this stuff on my way home from work, and then just shoving the bag into the refrigerator because the phone was ringing when I walked in the door. My seatmate can't stifle her giggles. "That's your lunch?" she says. "Raw onions?"

So in the end, I'm sharing her lunch, which isn't really so bad. Carrot and cucumber sticks, and fresh pineapple along with the peanut butter sandwiches. She's got a quart of apple juice she shares with me, too. And then for dessert, she pulls out homemade chocolate brownies. That's where my political palate quits policing my diet and goes off duty—homemade chocolate brownies.

I'm about halfway through my second one when she comments, "You know, it's been scientifically proven that chocolate satisfies the same biological need in human beings that's met by having sex." She really knows how to ruin a chocolate brownie.

"Look," I say, "What is it with you and sex?"

"What is it with you and no sex?" she counters.

Maybe if I answer her seriously, this time, she'll quit. "My lover left me," I say. "Three years ago. And I'm just not interested in sex anymore." There. It's out. The whole story.

"Your lover?" she says, like she doesn't know what the word means. "You sound like she was the only one who ever was and ever will be, now and forevermore, Amen. What are you talking about?"

"I'm talking about my lover." I'm getting angry. "If I was straight and I'd been married, and I said, 'My husband left me,' you'd understand. Well, I'm divorced. I got hurt. I got betrayed. I got dumped. And even when we *were* together, we hardly ever had sex. She didn't like it either. I don't want to have sex. I don't want to think about sex. And I don't want to talk about it."

I seem to have finally gotten through. She finishes her brownie in silence, and I do the same. She licks the last crumbs off her long, brown fingers and asks, "Could I look at that copy of *off our backs* you brought?"

I hand it over. She opens right up to "For Single Women Only." Of course, I didn't bring anything else to read.

We finally pull into the Stadium-Armory parking lot. The lovers appear to be still getting dressed, under the covers. It creates something of a bottleneck in the aisle. Traffic kind of slows down at the point where everyone has to pass them by. It's a relief to be off the bus, flinging my backpack onto my shoulder and charging for the open sunshine. I'm not looking back, off to find my friends among the three hundred thousand or so people who got it together and caught earlier buses this morning.

But I can't find anyone I know. There are so many more people than the organizers expected, I can't even find a marshall. Remembering that they're called peace-keepers now doesn't help. I'm doing well even finding my state. That narrows it down to thousands instead of hundreds of thousands. I never do find my city.

On the bright side of things, I don't run into my ex-lover either. But everyone else is there: Holly Near. Whoopi Goldberg. Toshi Reagon. All in all, it's a pretty wonderful day. The sun is out the whole time, and I can't believe how many people came. I decide that next time, I might even want to be a peace-keeper or something. I never get close enough to see the stage, but I'm right under a speaker, so I can hear all the speeches. They're great. Nobody says a word about sex.

I know I need to leave to get back to the bus on time, but I hate to tear myself away. How I finally convince myself to is by thinking about the woman who sat next to me on the bus. I start thinking that on the trip back, it could go differently. We could just have a normal conversation. I could ask her where she lives and where she works and what other marches she went on, and stuff like that. I know I need to start meeting new people. Maybe I'm even ready to start going out again. Suddenly three years feels like long enough.

Pushing through the crowd, what's in my mind is the image of her sleeping, looking so open and gentle, and not like my adversary any more. She was so close I could have held her while she was sleeping. Then I think about her buttons, marching in a straight, unbroken row down the front of the shirt that was the color of the sea. My hand aches to finger their flat smoothness. I know it will be night before we're back from this trip. The sun's starting to set, even now. I should have picked up something to eat, but there's no time now. I wonder if she has any more chocolate brownies.

Naturally, it's the last minute when I'm scrambling to get back to my bus on time. I didn't count on the subways being so crowded they wouldn't even let anyone down onto the platform for twenty minutes. Of course, I don't remember where the bus is parked, so I'm wandering around the parking lot another twenty minutes before I spot it.

A cheer goes up as I board the bus. A double empty seat's waiting for me, and the seat across the way's empty, too. The lovers seem to have gotten sidetracked, which isn't surprising. They're probably off behind a bush somewhere, and don't have any idea what time it is. They've probably been there since early this morning, and never even made it to the march. I'm surprised they ever made it off the bus.

The bus captain says to the driver, "Only two more."

"Only two?" I hear myself asking. "But where's. . . ."

"Ginger? Didn't she tell you? She's staying for the civil disobedience tomorrow, and taking the train back on Tuesday."

Just then, another cheer goes up, and I look up in time to see the missing pair come straggling onto the bus, hand in hand, with sheepish but satisfied looks on their faces. One of them, in the leather boots, is a woman I've never seen before in my life. The other one, in the sneakers, is my ex-lover.

Generation Gap

Valerie Taylor

I never really looked at Anne Rafferty until she resigned.

I saw her every day, of course. Some grade-school principals sit at a desk and shuffle papers. Not Rafferty. She patrolled the halls, snooped into the washrooms and sampled the cafeteria food. You never knew when that monumental figure was going to loom up. Almost six feet tall, weighing about a hundred and eighty, sternly tailored, with a halo of white hair, you knew she was there and behaved accordingly. My first week in the third-grade room I heard some of the Rafferty legends. When a mean seventh-grade boy came at her with a switchblade she said, "Give it to me," and stood with her hand out until the kid dropped the knife on her palm and ran off blubbering. She never pressed any charges.

We could tell the day of the week by which of her five expensively tailored suits she was wearing. "Gray plaid — must be Tuesday." She was a mythical figure.

Now there had been a special assembly, with the head of the school board laying a gold watch on her and a Congressman speaking platitudes. School was dismissed at noon in her honor. I walked out slowly, not sure what to do — go home and brood, see a movie or have a drink somewhere. Since Dinah had left me for a younger and prettier woman, time was slow and heavy.

Going down the stairs ahead of me was an unmistakable figure loaded with half-unwrapped packages, among them a leather briefcase. As I waited for her to move out of my way, she turned her ankle or hit her toe on a riser — I couldn't see what — and fell. Not down the stairs but forward, hitting her leg against a step. I hurried to help her up, seeing blood ooze through her stocking. "Are you all right?" A stupid question.

"I seem to have done something to my ankle." She gripped the stair rail, looking less pained than surprised.

"Shall I call somebody?"

"No, no, I'll be all right." She took a step and made a face.

"I'll drive you home," I said.

She didn't object. We made it to the parking lot, slowly. "Lean on me."

"My dear, I'd topple you."

That made sense; I'm five-two and weigh ninety-eight pounds in a bikini. Anyway, I carried her stuff and we made it to the car, not talking.

I'd have expected her house to be elegant in a roomy old-fashioned way. It wasn't. It was a small cottage with trees and flower beds in the front yard. The living room had bookcases along three walls and a small table covered with more books. Rafferty sat down in the wing chair. A Persian cat jumped out of a smaller chair and gave me a suspicious look. I glanced around for something to comment on. On the shelf over the fireplace was a studio portrait of a rather beautiful woman, her fair hair cut in 1960's style.

Rafferty said, "Alison. We were together thirty-seven years."

Well, of course, I'd wondered. To her generation, cast-iron tailoring spelled Career, not Dyke, and it is not true that it takes one to know one. With a woman my own age — thirty-two — I might have guessed, but there was that damned generation gap. At seventy you're more or less neuter anyway. I hadn't given the matter much thought. I didn't say anything.

Rafferty said, "She died of cancer."

How do you answer a flat-out statement like that? I said, "I'd better take a look at that ankle. It's swelling some."

Rafferty said with a malicious twinkle, "You sound like a camp counselor."

"I have been. Anyway, I have a first aid merit badge from my Girl Scout days." That was meant to be funny, but it didn't register. "It would be easier if you were lying down."

Her bedroom was, predictably, neat and bare. Nothing on the dressing table but a comb and a small book with a marker in it. She lowered herself onto the bed. I thought, "If she's wearing panty hose, this is going to be embarrassing." But wouldn't you know, she had on regular stockings, service weight, hooked up to some kind of a corset. I got the stocking off and touched her ankle gently. There was no lump — usually a sprained ankle swells up like a cantaloupe.

I said, "I think it's only strained. It ought to be all right if you put an Ace bandage on it and don't walk around much."

She said, "I can see you were a good Girl Scout."

I grinned, remembering. "Not very. I got kicked out when I was sixteen. For immoral behavior."

"With a young man?"

"With a girl."

You could have cut the silence with a knife. Then she raised herself up on an elbow and said, "Yes, that's the way it is. I'd forgotten — it was all so long ago. A long time now."

There was sadness in her voice, and it made me sad too. I said angrily, "Why should it be? There's no date on love. Or sex, either." I was furious at myself as soon as I said it. You don't go around telling hungry people that there's plenty of food in the world.

Only why did I assume that she was hungry? It was a note in her voice, a mellow cello voice, and a look in her eyes.

Her answer took my breath away. "That's nonsense. A young woman like you, for example, you wouldn't go to bed with anyone my age. The old ones are all dead, or in retirement homes, or they have someone. There is no percentage in being old."

"I don't see why not. People go on doing everything else, why shouldn't they make love as long as they feel like it? It used to be different. Now the generation gap has closed."

She lay back on the pillow. I could *feel* her thinking. Finally she said, "Will you help me get out of this damned outfit? If I'm going to be laid up, I might as well be comfortable."

She had on, can you believe it, a slip and a large bra with bones in it, and a cotton undershirt like kids wear. I haven't seen so many clothes on anyone since my grandma died. And a girdle, and cotton panties, and the other stocking. I helped her undress, very tactfully, putting a nightgown over her head before I took off the corset. Her dresser drawers seemed to be full of neat clean unsexy clothes, all neatly folded.

Her body astonished me. She was big, of course, but proportioned like the Venus de Milo. Those old Greek statues wouldn't make it today, I suppose. Her skin was smooth. Before I thought, I said, "You have a good body. You must take care of yourself."

"I eat sensibly. And walk a lot." She sounded embarrassed. At a bet, nobody except her doctor had ever looked at her since Alison died.

She asked abruptly, "Do you have a lover?"

"She walked out on me three weeks ago," I heard the bitterness in my voice. Three weeks of hoping that Dinah would come back, trying to make the vibrator seem like a person, picking up a couple of girls in bars — a whole lot of nothing. As somebody said, there is absolutely nothing like a dame. No substitutes.

I started to feel a tenderness for this woman with the massive breasts and column-like legs. And underlying the tenderness was something else. Something I would have liked to think over, because it seemed preposterous.

She said, "You don't find my body repulsive?"

"No. No, it's attractive in a—" What? Adult? Mature? Queen-size? I gave up. "I like it."

She lay still. There were tears in her eyes. Suddenly I knew how she felt. I said, "I might even seduce you, if you wouldn't mind."

She chuckled. "Well, I couldn't run away. I'm at your mercy."

I took her hand in mine, a large hand, with the nails cut short and not polished. It felt alive and, yes, electrical. She gripped my fingers. It was a kind of communication, as if currents of understanding were flowing between us.

One thing I learned from Dinah was not to hurry. She liked to make love slowly, as if savoring some wonderful food. I don't know how long we sat with our hands exchanging wordless messages, but it was a while. Then I turned back her gown and looked at her. Like a Greek statue, yes. I wanted to see her naked, but didn't want to alarm her. Later, I thought.

Her genitals were large, like the rest of her. Her clitoris was the biggest I ever saw, firm and upright. There's a theory that this little source of joy is a residual penis, a theory I'd always laughed at — who needs it? Now I could believe it.

I said, "You have a wonderful clit. Can I touch it?"

Mine, I might mention, is small and hooded but very responsive. Dinah once said it was like a pink pearl in a little rose-colored oyster. I left hers for future consideration, pulled myself up to the head of the bed and kissed her on the mouth, (I'm an old-fashioned type.) Her lips were crinkly and smooth at the same time; they clung to my mouth as a moth will cling to your finger. It was a long kiss, and by the time it was over I was getting wet and warm and excited, ready for whatever was going to happen.

I slid down in the bed and addressed myself to that magnificent clitoris, which seemed to have a life of its own. It responded as if it had been waiting a long time — and I guess it had. I circled it with my fingers, and then my tongue took it into my mouth and concentrated on it. Little sounds from Rafferty indicated that she was liking it. I moved a little and ran my tongue across her labia, and then inside.

I think it was Henry Miller who described his lover's cunt as a large room furnished with chairs and sofas and lamp tables. This one was like that. On a grand scale. I explored it thoroughly. By the time I came — I do sometimes, without being touched — I had forgotten everything else. Until I heard a cello whisper. "Tissues dry up as people age. I won't get very wet."

I mumbled, "Doesn't matter."

"I just want you to know something is happening. Didn't think it could."

It sounded so formal, and so apologetic, I almost laughed out loud. But too much was going on. I went back to the feast she had spread out for me.

I don't know how long this went on. The sunlight streaks on the wall had lengthened and shifted by the time she shuddered and moaned. I moved up beside her and put an arm across her, laying my head on her shoulder. She reached down and pulled off my damp panties, dropping them on the floor. She was more the type to fold things neatly over a chair.

By this time I'd have responded to a gnat's wing or the footstep of a fly. Her fingers knew exactly what they were doing. Maybe making love comes back to you, like riding a bicycle. I felt myself sail up through the ceiling and come down in a wonderful place where I had seldom been — not with my first teen-aged lover, not even with Dinah.

The only bad thing about making love is that it has to end. Like eating a wonderful meal — you reach a point where you can't hold another bite. We were both sleepy and happy by this time. At least, I was happy, and she looked it. We lay sort of folded together, still partly dressed, our hands on each other's flesh as the feeling receded. I dozed. Then woke to find her looking at me. She said softly, "I'd like to look at you."

I dropped my clothes, what little there was to drop, and stood hamming it up, turning like a model or a strip-tease artist. My body is all right. Not great, you understand, but all right, even if I do take a B-cup. I said, "We haven't had any lunch. Shall I fix something?"

Rafferty shook her head. "No. I want to lie here and think for a while. I think I can get around with the furniture to hold onto. Will you come back tomorrow?"

"To see how your ankle is doing?"

"That too."

"You couldn't keep me away."

She watched me dress. We kissed, and I turned to leave. As I reached the door, she said, "I'm embarrassed about something."

"I'm sorry."

"Not that. The thing is, what do I call you? I know your name is Judith," she said quickly, "of course I've read your folder, but what do I call you?"

"Oh," I said airily, "Judy, or Jude, or Darling, or whatever you want to. I shall call you Anna." Nonchalantly, as if nothing could be simpler.

She sat up in the bed and looked at me. "I'm not very good at first names," she said.

I put my hand on the knob. "Well," I told her, "that's the generation gap." And closed the door quietly behind me.

She Made Me Wait

Margaret Sloan-Hunter

She made me wait . . . for three weeks. Each kiss left a hurting passion; anticipation meant a constant throbbing between my legs. She told me, repeatedly, how wet I made her. I changed underwear twice daily. It was that real. It was that sensual. It was that heated. We could have done it on the first night. She mostly had; if she wanted them, then she would have them. But, she made me wait. I was that important to her.

On Thursday, we decided we would stay together the following Saturday night, after a concert. Those three days were painful and electric. My clit stayed hard; I felt the whole world was watching. During the concert she held my hand and traced my fingers. Each digit tingled. Without looking at me, she slowly and deliberately ran her polished nails up and down my arm, lightly, making the tiny, black hairs on my arm stand erect. She knew exactly what she was doing. Once, she turned to me and closed her full mouth over my lips. In her ear, I told her we would leave at the intermission. We did.

In my bed, the shyness and nervousness melted like candle wax heated by an orange flame. Through the sheet, I ran my hand over her form and felt her shapely hips and thighs . . . and her butt — the hallmark of the black woman. I had to see her naked. I had to see that round ass that had often been covered with denims, or a skirt or dress, but never with panties. Each time she had walked from me, I had stared intensely at her behind, always wanting to grab it; to squeeze it; to press myself into her. I pulled the sheet back and rubbed all over her and realized how innocent newness can make one feel. I introduced her body to my touch. Her hips moved in response. Her beautiful brown ass tightened. Anita was singing about rapture on the tape. Rhythm was not going to be a problem.

She had told me once that she did not like penetration. It did nothing for her. I had smiled. I knew that would change. The smell of her wetness filled the room. Her dark nipples were hard, like my clit. For three weeks, I had fantasized how slowly I would make love to her. In the face of reality, and pussy, vows can quickly be disregarded.

I ate her immediately, gobbled her up, wasted no time. I was hungry for her. I was on the edge of some new discovery, not just about her. It was mostly about me. In a rapture of sexual experience, you come to believe that you have experienced it all; that there can be no *new* feeling, simply a new partner. But now I was being introduced to sensations and sensual feelings that felt like snow in the center of July. As she arched her back, she sucked in her breath, and came into my face. I smiled, still tasting her. It had begun.

I climbed up next to her. My mouth smelled like she tasted. She licked my chin and smiled. My hand roamed down her chest, over her soft stomach and thighs, and I cupped my hand over her groin. I wanted her so badly, I forced myself to slow down. I wanted exact and detailed memories; the stuff of which great fantasies are made.

My fingers found her hole; open, with little resistance. She sucked them up into her. She begged me to go deeper. My steady, in and out rhythm made her curse under her breath in a gentle way. She responded with every thrust; she received each stroke as a necessary rite. No words were spoken, then the sounds of her quickened breathing, her moans, her juices flowed in the night.

☆　☆　☆

She wanted me on top of her. She knew I would come that way. She said she wanted to be under my big, black, ready body. She wanted to feel my power; my energy; my passion. I locked myself easily in place, on top of her. Our hips moved in time with each other, natural, easy, like a juicy prayer. I rocked back and forth, in and out, talking low in her ear. She responded with moans and her own words of passion. We said things that only black women can say to each other in the dark . . . in bed. That time of the miracle, when assumptions are necessary.

We were nothing less profound than two colored girls fucking and dripping, talking nasty and breathing hard and moving in syncopated sexual ecstasy. She grabbed my nappy dark hair with her gentle fingers and our eyes opened to each other in the stark realization that we were about to exchange trusting, wet explosions.

It was beginning, again.

Dearest Ann

Carolyn Gage

Dearest Ann,

I think the world for women is very hard, and very cold, and most of all dry. And we are meant to be wet. We are marsh creatures. And if this is not appropriate, if this is not mutual, if this is not WISE of me, then I am, as you remember, the one who lives with nothing to lose, so I am the one to take the chances. And if I have the feelings in my heart — misguided, or self-deluded, or whatever, but if I have the feelings to write something wet to a woman . . . well, I will take my chances.

But I so much regret the lack of honesty in New York, and the incomplete gesture, that I need to return to the scene and fix it. If you don't mind. You had reached up for the stick where I was putting flowers while I made small talk, all the time feeling the sexual tension between us growing and growing. And your hand came too close for me to stand not touching it, and I reached out and took it, and I was aware that my hands are not as lovely as yours, and I was frightened that you would not want me to hold your hand, but I just had to anyway. And I touched your beautiful smooth ivory fingers as they lay on my knee. And I told you how beautiful your hands were and you said my eyes were beautiful , and I lay back to feel my head against your breasts, and I remember my cheek was on your name tag, which seemed especially precious because it had your name on it, and I reached up and put my hand on your breast, and I thought my heart would stop, because it was such a tender and beautiful and gentle curving breast, like some dear creature in the forest. And I wanted to cry, because you were so beautiful. And then . . . and this is the moment I wanted to feel you touch me . . . this is the moment I should have told you.

And I would have told you that I was a survivor of incest and that I was unable to endure being touched without going into some place mentally which was very safe, and that I wanted to stay with you when you touched me. And that I had never told anyone that before, because frankly they don't notice and frankly I'd just as soon go into my world. But here is where I would pick the needle up and put it down in a different groove, and I would tell you, and of course, I would start crying, which is what I would do, because I would be so scared you wouldn't want to deal with somebody like me. And then when I told you, and I told you that I didn't know how, or even if it was possible, but that I wanted to be touched by you, that I would rather stay with you, even it was only for something very simple, than to make love with you and be wherever it is I usually go. And I would cry again, because of what has been done to me. (And it is a terrible thing when your own body is taken away from you . . . as it has been from so many of us . . . fat, thin, tall, short, older, etc. etc. What would it be if we loved our bodies? It would be war, of course. So we don't.)

But anyway, you would have held me and let me cry, and I would have stopped being so scared, and the woods which was without question participating in our rendezvous - if not actually conspiring - would do this thing with time, so that time would stop while I lay in your arms, and all the years of fears would heal up, like in time-lapse photography, when they show the flower actually opening. I remember seeing films of this in travelogues in Virginia, which my grandmother would take me to. I never got tired of watching those flowers bloom. It was like watching someone open presents, or doors on the advent calendar. And anyway, this is what would happen in your arms. And the sun would hold back until it was finished. And then, very slowly I would take your hand, and learn it. I would learn it by heart, as if I were blind, as if I would have to reproduce it exactly for the salvation of the world. I would touch it all over, I would trace the length of the fingers and the little U spaces at the base of each finger. I would learn it by heart.

And then I would move this lovely hand to my face and touch it to my face like Helen Keller. And I would kiss your hand, the palm, the fingers, the finger tips. And I would put my tongue in the little U's and lick between your fingers, imagining it was between your legs. And then you would lean over and look at me, because that is something lovers rarely do, because they can't really love you, so they don't. But you would look at me, with complete honesty, and I would look at you, and there wouldn't be the shadows and evasions, the little corners of criticism and censure. We would look at each other like two women who want to make love to each other. And then you would kiss me, and that very slowly, because there are land mines planted all over my body by the fathers, and you have to touch lightly at first and determine if there is a mine before you put your full weight on the area. And you can always tell when you hit one, because of the fear or the pain on my face, a sudden flight. And then you have to back up, and deactivate it and then go on. Which is why you have to kiss me very gently and very slowly. You never know where they have buried them.

But we get through it. You help me reclaim my body, and I am able to kiss you, not like a woman in the movies, but like the woman who owns her mouth. And I kiss you and we kiss and it's so sweet and so gentle and so long and so loving that I feel it run through my whole body, and I raise up my breasts to touch you. And I lift up your sweater and your shirt, so that I can see your breasts and feel them, and you sit up, take off your shirt and sweater and I look at your breasts. They are among the loveliest things in the forest. And I reach up and touch them. And you bend over me so that I can kiss them, one then the other. And you push my sweater up and touch my breasts. And of course they are mined. And I start to cry again and you remember. But you don't get annoyed or scared. You just give me a minute to catch up. And I take your lovely hands which are on my breasts, but I can't feel them of course. And I hold them, I hold them on my breasts, but I can't feel them. And I cry because I can't feel them. And I cry because maybe I never will. And the woods are angry at what has been done to me, and you are sad, and there is a great storm of feeling swirling around us . . . all the sadness and the frustration and the rage and the terror. And you lay your face on my breasts which aren't mine anymore. And this is not the way the fantasy was supposed to go . . .

I was going to write this incredibly wet letter to you, and it was going to be something for you, but in looking at it, it's all about me, as usual. And I'm sitting here crying, because it's like a prison, and I get very blue about it. And I can't even write a credible fantasy.

I make love fine, or at least I always thought I did. But anymore I have to ask just how real it is to give when you can't really receive. And what kind of a lover wouldn't notice that. And then I get very sad, but then I think, well, Carolyn, my, my, my look at how you've grown just in these few months. Look at how honest you are. You can be proud of that.

And I'm happy to be honest with you, because that is a compliment to you. You are the kind of person who deserves honesty, who inspires it. And that is why I feel like I love you. You have brought some very brave qualities out in me.

And if this isn't exactly the wet letter I set out to write, I can't say I'm sorry. I can't lie to you. And it is actually a very wet letter, it's just that the secretions all happened in my eyes instead of your cunt, which is where I wanted them to happen.

But as I said when I started, it's an awfully dry world for women, and we are marsh creatures. Take what kind of wet I can give you, because anytime a woman gives her lubrication, it is a precious river of life in this fucking desert rubble. I wish, I wish, I wish I could write you the letter I wanted to. You have touched my heart, Ann. Thank you.

      Love and girl tears,

————

"Dearest Ann" is excerpted from a longer collection, "The Ann Papers."

Time

Stephanie (C. S.) Henderson

Day.

An altar to my failure — the 9 × 12 manila envelope, the letter of rejection; the silent typewriter.

I sit in the leather armchair — folded, closed.

It is 5 to 6. In the next fifteen minutes I will hear the squish-plop of your sandals as you run up the stairs; hear your keys jangling toward the lock.

You will wait for the kiss, for the welcome home, and I will not be able to give.

You open the door.

I want to run to you and hold you close, touch My Reality.

But the hole in my stomach has sharp, pointy teeth, and I am afraid if I reach out to you, it will gnaw at my soul and swallow.

My tears leap at your arrival. They escape from my eyes where they hid from my heart. I want to speak but . . . I am a stutter, I am a moan.

And our Love without words draws you close to me.

Gently, deliberately, you cup my chin in four fingers and catch my tears with your thumb.

I raise my eyes to yours.

"They hated it!" I choke.

"They have no class," you smile.

"They tore it to shreds," I cry.

"We can send it to someone else."

"IT'S NO GOOD!" I scream and slap your hand away, and get up and flee from your closeness.

I go stand by the window. You come up behind me do not touch, but feel me.

"I think you are . . ." you whisper.

"I . . . HURT!" I wrench the words from my throat. Then, I am in your arms, sobbing, releasing. You wait until I am still . . .

31

"I know."

Night.
Rain.

Soft and light like a lullaby.

And we are the only two people left in the world—here, tonight, there are no ghosts—there is only you and me. And the quiet is solid . . . physical. The hush of anticipation hovers.

I am nude. I am covered by one sheet as I wait. I feel the pressure of your knee on the bed as you slide in close beside me.

We lie . . . like spoons.

I feel the pleasure of your breasts against my back, Your nipples like fingers between my shoulder blades. I can feel the heat as it rises from your mound; your hairs tickle where the bottom of my twat lays open—salivating for your touch.

You stroke the pink slit that is the Mouth to My Soul; then you moan.

Juices secrete from my wettest walls.

They baste your finger. Entry in me is smooth. I clutch at your finger with my vagina muscles . . . and we move like ripples, like ribbons in the wind.

Where is your hand? I reach behind me and grasp it in mine. Guide it—kneading, exploring, tweaking the bud you have coaxed from my breast. I take your palm and bring it to my mouth, making small circles in it with my tongue.

And there is no sound but the rain. And the wet, sloppy noises of your finger inside me.

I have lost track of who is who, here. Because I cannot reach you, I have made your palm into another orifice. I return each of your movements inside me with my tongue. Your breaths are short and quick. Your ballet inside me has become a jig. The sweat from your breasts slick down my back—and I am needing you, and loving you, and wanting you. And I hear the rain, I feel the rain, and I am the rain . . . and you are the Earth that absorbs me.

Your fingers close to my face stretch, expand, following the tensing of your body behind me.

You have raised your pelvic mound close to mine so that there is a finger in my vagina and yours. I feel the small gem of your clit close to my labia. The friction—the just barely touching—sends my vulva into convulsions.

The room is full of love sounds — sounds of mucus. The creak of the bed, hard gasps, shallow breaths; the sound of vaginal juices being stirred, the slap of sweaty bodies together; sloppy wet kisses cover each of our bodies, my name . . . and yours — muffled, murmured, moaned — whispered.

"Fuck me. Love me, fuck me, love me. Please . . . please."

You extract your finger so abruptly from inside me that a little scream escapes.

Gentle hands guide my body around. The sound of movement (it is so hard to see now), away from me, over me. I feel your arms on either side of my shoulders, your knees on the inside of mine. You lower your body onto mine, slowly, tease me, then we touch —

Like steam.

A long sigh as we are joined together. There is a feeling of wholeness. There is no separation here — we are at the place that we share.

I am no longer Rain. You have sealed the spaces between drops with your closeness. Together, we are one slow swell. Our bodies in the same rhythm as we rise, peak, spread as we touch shore.

Kisses.

Shoveling Kisses. Kisses excavating passions; kisses that draw you deep into my throat where I swallow you, a warm liquid in my belly that spreads through my loins and comes out of my twat . . .

Touch me — there.

Those lips have closed in your absence. The key lies in your hands. Stroke them gently, friendly, 'till they open wide and gush at your return.

So many Life fluids here: the rain outside, the sweat, the saliva. Your hair is matted to your face by your sweat. The damp sheets below us, the river inside us, the slickness of our bodies as you slide, down.

Lower.

Oh, yeah, that's it. Is that finger or tongue — you, so adept at magic — with what would you dazzle me tonight?

I wait, expectantly, on the edge of the ledge, for . . . Tongue. Flat like a cobra head. The tip, muscley hard, touches the bottom of my uterus and lifts love juices to my clit, and every nerve ending stands up and shouts.

This is my Daily Bread.

I am a jolt. I am a scream.

You murmur "sweet sweet" over and over, as if waiting for an answer, as if waiting for an echo, and it comes as I spread myself wider to you. I want to capture you, I want to inhale you, want you to be in my body with me. I want to feel you underneath my skin.

And we are a clock that's been wound too tight. I feel us coiling, tighter, tighter. I dig my fingers into your flesh, feel the beginning of Frenzy. I am almost there wondering will you come with me and you (who knows me better than myself) wrest your mouth away from my pool.

Then you mount me; we ride, we trot, we gallop . . . OVER THE LEDGE. A descent into ascension.

We are the Balloon let go in inflation, and we rocket off walls, onto ceiling, then floor.

And the Love That We Made leaks into a puddle that tomorrow will be a small stain on the sheets.

Afterwards, soft sounds come easy. The world outside creeps back into our peace. I huddle into the warmth of your body—one hand touching the place where you touched me, the other touching where I touched you.

Sleep.

Day.

An altar to our passion. A cup of coffee, the paper, a rose.

I treat myself to the pleasure of your waking, watch how your body slowly comes to life. You turn, sensing I am watching, catch sight of my offering by my side.

"I know you don't expect me to be able to walk," you stretch.

"No. Not this morning, anyway."

"C'mere," you beckon, your voice a tease.

"Gladly," I reply, and go to your side.

As I put down the tray I watch you.

You will do as you've done so many times before: pick the coffee up, blow twice, then sip. Put it down then raise the rose up to your cheek. You are so familiar and that thought comforts me—

Not like publishers or life.

I stroke your face with the back of my hand and slip my robe knot undone. I glide my fingers over your body and let the robe fall to your floor.

I drop to my knees, kiss the joint at your thigh.

"No typing today?" you ask as you spread your legs and welcome me inside.

I kiss the Canal at the place of your birth. "No," I murmur into its chasm. "No. At least, for a while."

All We Really Are Is Open

Sherry Thomas

We became friends at meetings, something which doesn't often happen to me. She lived on the same road as I so we sat talking late into the night in her driveway or mine. One night, I spoke to her of my fears — that I couldn't be close to anyone, didn't know how to share, was afraid to be vulnerable or open. I was crying and she put her arms around me, kissed my forehead, touched me. The next week, we sat in her driveway and she told me about wanting to get close to women again, about a woman she had loved fourteen years before, about her children, about living without a lover the last two years. Our hands touched; we kissed, first tentatively then passionately. Later I laughed. "Two teenaged adolescents," I said, "making out in a car!" Then I started to cry. "Damn it, I'm afraid of you, of us. I'm afraid of getting close, of being friends, of making love. Go on, go into the house. I have to get home tonight."

The next week there was a meeting at her house. I arranged for someone to milk the goats the next morning, and left for the meeting early, driving alone. "I wondered if you'd have the sense to come alone," she said. "I'm glad." That night we slept together, touched each other's naked bodies, gently, feeling, testing. Getting more courage, she touched my clitoris with her finger, rubbed me until I felt pleasure and excitement. Following, I touched her there too.

"Why can't I make love to you?" she asked, nights later. "What do you mean?" I said, naive, embarrassed. "I don't kiss you; I don't touch you freely, unconsciously. It's all so polite," she wailed. "I don't know why I'm so inhibited." "I'm afraid I'll bore you," I answered. "You are older, more experienced, more free. I've never liked making love. I'm afraid I won't want you to touch me. I don't know how to touch you; I'm afraid I can't make love with you."

One day she said to me, "I try not to tell lies in bed." "I don't think I've ever not told lies in bed," I answered. "I only do what I really want to; I want you to do only what you really want to," she said. It sounds so simple, I thought. And with a momentary flash of confidence, I forgot that I didn't know how. Loving her, I loved her body. I touched her freely with my hands, exploring, caressing. I kissed her mouth, her ears, the curve of her neck, the hollow between her breasts, her cunt. I loved how she was all curves and hollows. My own body felt pleasured and moved by our touching. "Oh, my dear," she said. (No one has ever called me "my dear," though I've wished they would.)

"I like fucking," she said. "I don't," I said. "It hurts and I feel alienated and I don't have orgasms." But I also thought, I will touch her wherever she wants. I put one finger tentatively inside her warm, good, home, womb. "You can put your whole hand inside me," she said. "No," I said. "You can," she said. "It's because of all those babies," I said. "No, it isn't," she said, and I slid two more fingers in. My hand moved, turned, plunged, wiggled inside her. I floated on ocean waves, rocked in the salty wet warmth of the womb. My body trembled all over and I cried. She sighed and laughed and cried out and came.

"I can only get one finger inside you, you're so tight," she said. I was tensing, making myself come. "Relax," she said. I did. I began to fly, loose, at peace, pleasured; she kissed my clitoris, touched my cervix. "Do you want to come?" she asked. "Oh no, never," I said, flying higher and higher, not wanting to land. Later I remembered she had said, "Relax," after years of tightening up. Tightening, a good tight cunt is what a man wants said Miller and Lawrence and countless jokes about obstetricians and episiotomies. Tight so I would come quicker, tense to get my orgasm and all that foreplay over with so we could get down to real business. "Relax," she said, and I flew.

One night I held her, kissed her; suddenly for the first time ever I wanted a penis, wanted to take her, to possess her totally. "Desire is not love," she said later. Tired, I still wanted all of her.

Looking at her beautiful breasts, her belly, her tiny thin body one night, I remember how I used to envy men touching mine. I used to have fantasies that I was them making love to myself. Loving her, I love myself more. Together, I love our freedom.

"Only do what you want to do," she said. But I am learning that the hard part is not doing but knowing what I want. Do I want to touch her? hold hands? stroke her hair? kiss her? passionately? lie together naked touching bodies? suck her breast? touch her vagina? put my hand inside? excite her? excite me? Do I want to stroke her clitoris? Sometimes we lie together side by side, a half an inch apart, feeling the presence of each of us and both of us, feeling if we want to move and how.

Learning to be honest with her is learning to know more and more what I feel myself, is infinitely harder than I imagined.

My lips at her breast, child lover, wondrous. "You've finally learned to suck," she said. I laughed. "My mother never let me nurse." "Let's see if we can suck each other's at the same time," she said. (We can.)

I wanted her, not to possess her, but for her to know all of me. I wanted to hold her inside of me. I was open and she entered me. Again, the ocean waves and the joy of them breaking through me.

My fingers inside her, I began to wiggle them, then changed to an undulating rhythm. She vibrated with the rhythm of my fingers, my shoulder, my body. I tried all kinds of motions with my fingers; sometimes rotating, thumping against her vagina, its walls tight like a drum, sometimes plunging in and out like a penis, though I like that less. Sometimes deep, I touched and caressed her cervix. "I love your hand," she said. "It does so much."

My friend Carolyn wrote from far away, "What do you do when you have a crush on a woman and you don't know if she's open and she doesn't know if you're open?" I remembered an old copy of *The Furies* with an article on coming out. In very large type on page four it said, "I'm feeling very attracted to you and wonder if you'd like to make love?" The article suggested that until you get used to making overtures and being aggressive, you could always keep that copy of *The Furies* with you and when the time was right, hand it to your friend saying, "Page Four!" I dug through my old copies and sent that issue to Carolyn.

As I thought of things, I wrote Carolyn letters. "It's terrifying to make love with another woman," I told her. "They tell you it's so natural, just do whatever you like." But the first time, I suddenly thought, "What if she doesn't like what I like? What if I'm weird? Do I even know what I like?" With men there's such a gap, I can breeze through or fake anything because he is never going to know what I feel, experience what I experience. With him, I can mystify my experiences because the gap, the difference, the distance is the whole point. It's the union of the completely different separate beings that is exciting. But with a woman, it's the opposite; it's the sameness that's the excitement, the perfect oneness." And suddenly I wondered, "What if no other woman is like me?"

Another time I wrote, "Don't be surprised if you hate yourself after you start making love with a woman. After the first time, I went through months of feeling like a failure—about my work, my farm, myself, my relationships. Everything I did was despicable. Finally a friend said, "Do you think it's connected to sleeping with Kathy?" Connected with being separated from my husband, unloved and unwanted by any man, 'perverted', in love with a woman, independent, myself? Of course it was.

"I wish we had a language," I said. "We are so awkward when we talk. You say 'eat me'; I say 'kiss my cunt' — neither is right. 'Cunt' is a man's word; 'vagina' and 'clitoris' are so clinical; 'eat me' and 'touch me' seem embarrassed into generalities. I want a language to love you in."

One night, curled together, each of us inside the other, moving slowly through infinite pleasurable space, I thought, "the joy of homosexuality is to be both receptive and active. Being entered is a state of total receptiveness — if it's not passive submission. Entering is an act of union. Together we can experience both or either, as we choose to. All modes are open to us, a thousand between each pole."

"Can you do that with a man — be both active and receptive?" I asked. "I have . . ." she said, then pausing, "No, not the same. With you I am uncovering my aggressive self. I don't know what it will be like when I sleep with a man again." For her being active was the place of growth. Though it surprised me, making love to her came easily to me, with joy and abandon, my whole body pleasured and excited by our sharing. But being receptive was new to me, a revelation, transforming old patterns of submitting to another's needs into real acceptance of my body and her loving. In homosexuality, entering is an act of love; in any sexuality, it can be.

"Don't touch me," I said. "I want to be left alone." Lying on my side with my back to her, hunched against the pain and cold, every muscle tight, guarding against even the most gentle and innocent contact. I heard her crying and felt angry. "What have I done?" she asked. "It's not you, it's me," I answered. "I'm hating myself so much I can hardly stand to live in my own body and I don't want anyone else to touch me." "I love you, all of you," she said. "I know, but I can't bear to be loved." She turned away from me, sad and a little hurt. We slept with those three inches of badly needed space dividing us. I awoke less frozen, a little able to feel my fears. She awoke smiling, "It's far out that I could let go enough to sleep." Weeks later she said, "I'm going to sleep in the other bed tonight. I feel like being alone." And I could remember clearly that need for solitude and separation and could let that first impulse to feel hurt and rejected pass through me.

One day during one of my depressions, she asked, "What are you afraid of?" "I'm afraid you'll get sick of all my pain and fear and craziness and not want to see me anymore." "What I get sick of," she said, "is your shutting yourself off from me. You imagine what I might feel and then believe it's what I do feel. You judge your feelings and hate yourself for having them and me for seeing them. I want to be with you. It doesn't matter to me what you have to do, but *do it*! Let yourself be yourself."

"Do you want to come?" she asked me often. "Yes," I said unashamedly. "It doesn't matter," I said honestly. "Tell me what you want," I asked her sometimes, unembarrassed by my lack of prescience. "Loving is not being ashamed to be whatever I am," she said. "I love you," I said. "I love you," she said. "I know."

"Make me come," she said, putting my hand on her clitoris. "I don't feel comfortable with my hand anymore," I said, "I'm afraid I'll irritate you or I won't turn you on at all. I can't find the right place to touch; I don't know what to do." "Will it make you feel bad if I masturbate?" she asked. "I feel so bad now, it would be a relief." "Stay close to me," she said, "don't go away." I felt strange there beside her, tense at my failure to give her what she wanted, twinges of guilt, but also relieved — that we could say what we wanted and that we weren't so dependent on the other for satisfaction. Lying beside her, my arms around her, I remembered furtively masturbating when other lovers had fallen asleep, to relieve the aching tension of my body. And I felt a flood of love for this woman, coming now to orgasm in my arms, for her ruthless honesty, for her tiny body and translucent rose-flushed skin, for the clarity of her spirit. My god, how I love her!

I had been making love to her for a long time. First touching her body, kissing her anywhere and everywhere; then sucking her breast and rubbing her feet; then licking her ear, kissing her mouth, touching her cunt. Then three fingers in her vagina, my whole body loose and free with pleasure. Then much later, my mouth on her clitoris, my hand inside her, both moving quickly, pressing deep. My breasts rub her belly and my vagina runs juices. She comes and I move my mouth away. Lying beside her, my body pressed tight against her, I move my hand slowly gently inside her. Later, my hand vibrating in waves inside her, my fingertips on her cervix, she began to come again. Then mouth on cunt, hand beating inside, both our bodies quivering with the rhythm, she comes and comes and comes. Tremors of pleasure run through my whole body — toes to head. And then in silence and peace, I kissed her eyelids and lips, gently. Curling next to her, already half asleep, I realized that she was crying. Hurt, frightened, not understanding, I finally asked "What's wrong?" "Being so passive makes me afraid," she said, "It's meant such bad things in my life and I start to hate myself." "I love you," I answered, "I feel such joy when I touch you and I want to give you pleasure." "I know," she said, "but I am afraid."

Her hand was inside me, drumming hard, beating wildly, my body loose, flowing with her. The pleasure became intense, up my vagina, through my belly, to the top of my head, to the tips of my fingers. Waves and waves of contractions flowed through my vagina, held her, united us. Then I was relaxed, at peace. "Will you write that there *are* vaginal orgasms?" she asked. "I don't know," I say. "It's not the same as a clitoral one." "An orgasm is a climax and a release," she said. "You felt that didn't you?" "Yes," I answered, "but completely differently. My favorite coming is when you touch me inside and out. But the more we make love, you know, the less I want to come at all! It's the being there I love."

One day, the father of her younger child came to visit, bringing his current lover and his mother. This visit was to introduce the child and his grandmother, an unfamily reunion fraught with all kinds of love energy and tension. As he entered, he bent and gently kissed her. I felt pain at the perfect beauty of that image, their fine-boned semitic faces, their clear, clear blue eyes. They were two of a kind. On the floor sat their child, looking like each of them. I suddenly felt intensely jealous of that child, who I lived with and was friends with and loved, because he was a tie between them that would last forever. They have a child. I felt a terrible mean desire to possess her that way too, to make her have my child. The intensity of the jealousy and the desire to bind her, to hold her, shocked me. Yet all the while I was at best anonymous, in that cozy, difficult family scene. To his mother I was "a friend" — one can present ones unmarried heterosexual lovers to one's mother (maybe) but definitely not one's homosexual lovers. Though he knew me and knew of our relationship, he never once looked at me directly, concentrating on the difficult communication between the child, his mother, his former lover and himself. His new lover was as jealous and as pained as I but more obviously possessive. Finally she turned to me and started chatting. We sat in the corner talking, like two wives. It took me a long time after they all left to remember clearly that our love was in the present moment strong and clear, making past and future and possessiveness irrelevant.

Another time, "I'm leaving; I can't stand it anymore!" I shouted, grabbing up my coat and the nearest sleeping bag. "You'd better not run away; I'm not going to come get you," she said, "I don't value pleasure any more than I do pain. What I care about is what's happening right now, not how it feels. You want to cancel me out — you want niceness, not ME." "Yes, I value pleasure more than pain. I don't want any more pain," I yelled, crying. "I hate you!" "I know," she answered, "I hate you too right now. So what?" I stood there angry for several minutes, caught up in the drama and unwilling to give up the role. Then I couldn't help myself: I smiled and put down the sleeping bag. "You tell me why you hate me and I'll tell you why I hate you," I offered. And we did.

Our friend Maureen said, "I just don't get turned on to women." "No, you won't 'just get turned on' to women," I answered, "until you've begun making love with a woman." It takes a long time to break down the patterns and images we've been taught forever. One day after I'd been making love with my first woman lover for several months, I realized that I was seeing women with new eyes, aware of their bodies, aware of their sensuality, aware of their whole beings. I wasn't the nymphomaniacal rapist that heterosexual women sometimes imagine lesbians to be. I was just very much alive to the possibility that sometime I might love one of my friends, or a woman met at a meeting somewhere, or a woman who was still a stranger on the street.

She touched my anus with her finger. "It's just another hole, you know," she said. One night, three fingers inside her vagina, pushing deeply, deeply, my fourth went in her anus, pushing deeply. I felt an anguishing, tearing kind of pleasure run all through me. Forbidden territory; deeper union. Desire and love were all confused within me. I wanted her. I wanted her to know more pleasure than she ever had. My thumb rubbed her clitoris too. "Oh honey, honey, honey, baby!" she cried out.

We were making love one day and I felt her finger go in my anus, very deep. The excitement in my vagina, in my whole body intensified. "Oh my god," I thought, "I'm going to shit." Then I realized I was just feeling her finger. Later I wanted to laugh — it felt very perverse and very funny to finally acknowledge that shitting can be pleasurable. "Oh no!" she said. "What?" I asked. "Fucking in the ass! We're like a couple of male homosexuals!" "Whatever feels good . . ." I said.

"Are you writing everything down?" she said. "People are going to think we're weird." "All we really are is open," I answered. "What's going to happen if we stop liking to make love?" she asked. "Do you only love me for my body?" I asked. And we laughed and hugged.

One night we went to bed exhausted but too full of nervous energy to sleep. I tossed and turned, tried counting sheep. She talked intermittently. "You know," she said, "it would be better if we just tuned into what we need to relax and did it, we can just fuck and go to sleep." We've got such exalted standards of lovemaking we've forgotten how to be simple when we need to be.

"Reading your journal turns me on," she said. "I want to go to sleep tonight," I answered. "What are you doing?" she asked. "Protecting yourself from the future? Changing what you will feel then by what you fear now? I didn't say anything about making love; I'm just about to go out and milk the goats." She's right, I thought as I built the fire. I still fear that my being honest will bring anger or rejection from my lover. So here I am, building walls between myself and the first person I've ever been honest with, in case I won't be honest when we go to bed, separating us over something that's happening only in my imagination.

As it happened, after we had cooked dinner and gotten the children to sleep and spent several quiet hours talking and reading, I wanted very much to make love with her, to be as close together as we could. Staying clear in the moment, not projecting into the future is something I have never done before. But within the moment there is infinite freedom to be anything I am.

Lying with her head in my lap, she said, "All my images are changing. When we were first making love, if I felt turned on, I would think 'I want to be fucked.' Now, I think 'I want my cunt kissed; I want your hand inside me.' I'm afraid I'm becoming a homosexual!" "I don't mind if you do," I answered. "I do," she said, "I want this freedom to lead to being more open, not more closed."

During a restless night, we woke several times to talk. "It's so hard to be near you, to touch you without becoming sexual," she said, "I wonder if that's why it's hard for lesbians to be affectionate — because we make love with our hands; our hands are sexual objects!" The next morning, I said, "It hurts me that you said we're not affectionate. I am. I love to hug you, touch you, rub your back." "I know," she said. "I was wrong about that. But the hands, what I said about hands was important. You love the thing that makes love to you — I love your hands, your arms, your mouth."

"I have something to tell you," she said. "What?" "You asked me to tell you," she said. "What?" I said. "I made love with Laurie last night," she said. "Well, I'm glad you can touch and love each other again," I said. "Is it really ok?" she asked. "When we are clear with each other, it doesn't matter what you do with any one else," I said. "You blow my mind," she said.

Sometimes I like the taste of her cunt, sometimes it scares me. When I like it, I cover her whole cunt with my mouth, sucking, licking, kissing. Mouths and cunts feel somehow the same, united in wetness and pleasure. I like to explore with my tongue the edges of her lips, the inside of her vagina, the tip of her clitoris. I like how she comes beneath my tongue, moaning and crying and laughing. I like how I come beneath her tongue, with a pleasure which is almost too much to bear.

We are both a little afraid of menstrual blood. Sometimes we feel desire and intimacy that makes a period irrelevant. Other times that knowledge that one of us has her period seems to inhibit us, to lessen desire.

The first time I found her blood beneath my fingernails, I felt a deep tenderness and love for our union. Another time, I felt excited at the feel and look of all that blood. "Blood sisters is what we are," I thought. "A tampax is like one more finger in the vagina," she said while making love to me. "Feels good," I answered. The first time I tasted her blood I felt scared, neither clearly excited nor repulsed, just scared. I still feel confusion now, as though my intellect fears what my body does not.

Away from her now on a trip, I'm finding it hard to be a celibate again. Walking down the street, I catch a smile from a man or woman and have a swift fantasy of making love. A little shocked, I have to laugh at my secret nymphomania. I feel happy about it too; having been frozen for so long, it's good to be a whole body person. One night I put two fingers inside myself and felt surprise: this doesn't feel familiar. I've come to know the feel of her vagina so well. I'm aware of all the differences in mine. I remember Sally telling me about a woman who photographed hundreds of women's cunts and no two were alike! Then forgetting thoughts, I felt those fingers inside me, moved them in waves, thumping them against my vagina. Oh joy! Learning to make love to her with abandon, I'm learning to make love to myself with more freedom too. No more "masturbation," this is love making. My whole body relaxes.

First published in *Country Women* magazine, April 1975.

The Dancer

Sabrina Sojourner

The first time I noticed her was actually the second time she was there. It's not that unusual for women to come into strip joints. But, the same woman two nights in a row, that's cause for notice. She had a couple of men with her. I don't remember if they were the same as the ones from the night before. I was curious. But, I really didn't think much more about it. Later, she would tell me that she kept hoping I would try and catch her eye.

That didn't happen until about a week later when she came by herself.

I was in the wings watching this new girl. She was auditioning. Cute but boring. So, my attention wandered to the audience. I was so surprised to see her standing at the bar with a drink in her hand. She was looking for a place to sit down. She was dressed differently, of course. Navy blue slacks and a lighter blue shirt open at the neck. She was also wearing a leather blazer-style jacket. She looked sharp. I liked how she moved through the crowd. Strong and sure of herself. It was as if she was daring any one to enter her space.

It was only as she planted herself in a spot down front, pretending to watch the dancer, that I remembered that that's what I needed to be doing. From that point on my attention was equally divided between her and the act. The more I looked, the more fascinated I became. She really was very good looking and I wanted to know, who is this woman? What does she do for a living? Could she really be here to see one of the dancers? Maybe, even to see me? Of course, she could be here to be picked up by a man. I laughed as I realized she had gotten my attention. Something no one had been able to do for a long, long time.

At one point, a waitress came over with a drink some one had bought for her. She merely nodded in the direction the waitress pointed. When the man came over and tried to join her, she handed him the drink and shooed him away. He left the drink and walked back to his seat, muttering. I could tell she was quite pleased with herself. We had quite a laugh about it later.

Since I was still in the wings when the next dancer started, Bobby came over to see what I was up to. I indicated her with my head. He studied her for a bit, then raised an eyebrow. He looked so funny, I laughed.

As he turned to leave, he whispered, "By the way, I heard her asking if you were working tonight when she was at the bar."

"Are you shittin' me?"

"Would I do that to you?"

I studied him for a moment and decided he was telling the truth. "Thanks, Bobby."

"Anytime, Sweetheart," he said ala Bogie.

I didn't give the signal for my music until I caught her eye. When she smiled up at me, I began my dance. And it was for her I danced. Every twist, twirl, back bend and dip. Every arc and swing of the arm and leg. Every shimmy. Every shake. I made eye contact only with her. We were no longer in a sleazy night club. I was performing a birth dance for the women of my tribe. Inviting the spirit of the child to come forth and meet her new family.

Her smile never faded. I liked her smile. It made her look younger, softer.

Back in my dressing room, I wrote a note inviting her backstage. Bobby looked at me with another raised eyebrow when I sent him to fetch her. But he went. You see, in the two years I've worked at Gus's, I'd never worked the crowds or accepted anyone into my room, much less invited someone back.

I wasn't sure I had enough time to put clothes on. So I just grabbed this yellow satin robe of mine. I also decided to wash some of my makeup off. It seemed like it was taking her forever to get back there. I kept giving myself a bad time for being so nervous. And I almost jumped out of my skin when there finally was a knock on the door. I took a deep breath, trying to regain some composure before opening it.

I couldn't believe my eyes when I saw the bouquet of balloons which greeted me.

"For you," she said.

"Oh. How wonderful! Won't you come in? Where did you find balloons?" They're great!"

"Down the street."

"Well, thank you. That was very sweet. What's your name?"

"Robyn."

"Robyn, I'm Clarissa. But you can call me Gypsy."

"I'd rather call you Clarissa."

Her saying that pleased me. "Okay! That'd be great. Please, sit down. Can I fix you a drink?"

"Sure. How 'bout scotch and water?"

"Scotch and water it is."

"I've got a question."

"'What's a nice girl like you doing in a place like this?' Sorry, I no longer answer that question."

"I don't blame you. There's no reason for you to have to explain your choices."

"I think I'm gonna like you, Robyn. So. What's your question?"

"What was so funny to that guy who brought me the note?"

"He didn't give you a bad time, did he?"

"No, no. He just seemed. . . . I don't know. Amused, I guess."

"Well, I don't work the crowds like the rest of the girls. And I've never let anyone back to my room for as long as I've worked here. There's been more than enough guys who've tried. You know. They slip Bobby $20 or $30 dollars, or more, to arrange an introduction.

"I used to have to match what they gave him to keep them out. Then, I don't know. Something changed. I think Bobby actually likes that there's at least one of his girls who doesn't fool around with the customers. Now, if any one tries, I don't know about it."

"Why do you call the women you work with 'girls'?"

"Women? Girls? the only difference is attitude. And we all know who we are. I like that I work with women. I like the sharing, caring and nurturing we offer one another. I use girls the way some women use sisters, because that's what they are to me — my family."

"So, I'm the first person to be invited to your dressing room."

We both laughed at the obvious change in subject.

"Yes, you are the first."

"Well, I'm honored."

"I'm honored that you accepted my invitation."

We sat in silence for a few minutes. Just smiling at one another. I, for one, was feeling a little shy.

"Would you like to go out?" Robyn asked. Then she laughed. "Go dancing?"

"Yeah! I would. It'll only take me a moment to change."

I had this urge to kiss her as I walked by. Instead, I brushed her face with my hand. Robyn caught my hand and kissed the inside of my palm. Doors flew open and windows popped up. A warm breeze moved through me. She leaned into the hug I gave her from behind, my arms around her neck.

"You smell good," whispered Robyn as she kissed me on the cheek. I kissed her forehead and walked behind the screen. I wanted to kiss her lips. To taste her. I smoothed my hands down my body and wondered what hers would feel like.

☆　☆　☆

Apparently, she was a regular at the club we went to. Robyn introduced me around, ordered our drinks and guided me to a table close to the dance floor.

"Do you really like to dance?" I asked.

"Yeah, I do."

"Good! Let's go."

Robyn was laughing as she followed me onto the dance floor. She really was a good dancer. And when she realized I wasn't going to hold back, she loosened up. It was great dancing with someone who could keep up with me.

When a slow song came on, she invited me into her arms. I snuggled close. I let her lead us in a two-step. It's my favorite way to dance with women. Pelvis against thigh. As if I needed any more help getting turned on.

It felt good being in her arms. It was a warm, safe spot. I felt her tenderness. The pounding of her heart echoing my own. The heat rising between my legs and radiating through my body, meeting the desire in her kiss on my forehead. The hunger for another's touch, for her touch, rose, awakened in my soul. It had been so long since I had let another close. I let anxious thoughts float on through. I wanted what Robyn had to offer. I wanted to give what I could give. I pulled her closer to me.

She kissed my neck and a shiver went down my spine. I wanted her closer. When our lips and tongues met, an electrical storm raged within me. Yes, this is what I wanted, what I had missed, the warmth of another searing through the pretense of propriety with the flick of a tongue.

Robyn rested her lips on my forehead and a wave of serenity washed over me. Gazing into her piercing blue eyes, they became clear, calm pools for me to swim in.

I took a deep breath and asked, "Would you like to take me home?"

We necked all the way to her apartment. In the cab, in the elevator, down the hall and through the door. Our tongues chased each other, danced a waltz, the minuet and the hustle. We nursed each other's lips, giggled and licked. I felt like I was about sixteen and discovering sex for the first time. I was ready to cut loose.

"Drink?" Robyn offered as she led me to the bedroom.

"Only if you're going to have one."

"Naw. I'm fine. I just want some more of those kisses."

Robin lavished my face and neck with kisses. She followed the collar line of my shirt with kisses. We undressed each other as we continued kissing and cooing and licking and sucking and tasting and teasing.

I felt myself melt into her and she into me as we lay skin to skin. The sun rose inside us, stretching its warming rays the full length of our bodies. Evaporating all worries, all concerns. Even my toes felt sexy as they played with Robyn's toes. We were wide open spaces. Limitless. Boundless. We were the sun radiating loving pride to all around us, bright, beautiful beacons, calling, "See us. Feel our warmth and joy. Share it. Take it."

As Robyn's hot mouth worked it's magic on my breasts, I became a sun nurturing another bright spirit. And in the giving there was receiving, the cycle being never ending. All loving, caring, nurturing beauty flowed through me and to me.

"It's all yours," I whispered.

Robyn moaned and the texture of her sucking changed. Elongated. Nibbling here. Licking there. She cupped my left breast with both hands, taking as much as she could into her mouth. It felt like it was all in her mouth. And the direct line between my breasts and my clit was overloaded with the passion of our pure female energy.

Robyn kissed her way to my ear, scooped me into her arms and rolled us onto her back. Our tongues pranced, glided and bobbed. She caught and teased my bottom lip as if it were a nipple. And my nipples ached for the feel of her tongue and lips. The last door to me opened wide as Robyn skied her tongue off my chin, down the slope of my neck. A shiver shattered any remaining anxieties as she captured my burning nipples. The coolness of her mouth soothed the ache.

Her strong arms moved me forward bathing my tummy with her tongue. She positioned herself and lowered my sex to her face. We both moaned as we touched. The vibration from her moan threatened to break me loose.

"Slow down," I whispered.

Her tongue paused on my clit.

"That's too intense! Ohh, yess! That's it. On the sides. Ohhh! Yesss! Just like that!"

Her tongue moved around my clitoris, the length of my pelvis and back again. Lingering inside my vagina; slurping my juices. The gestures were indulgent. Unhurried. In rhythm: Long lick. Linger. Long lick. Tease. Long lick. Linger. Long lick. Tease. The rhythm opened me. I was flowing like a river. Feeling energies wanting to escape my banks. Readying for transformation. I wanted to hold back, but the urge was too strong. I needed, wanted to let go. To climb the spiral and dance the dance.

I grabbed Robyn's hands to ground my body, to remind my conscious mind that I was safe. And holding her hands tightly, my soul rose to meet the fire spirit of passion. Entwined, we danced me to ecstasy.

The Queen of Hearts

Hannah Blue Heron

You might say it all began in August of 1945. It was also the month of Hiroshima. I was horrified at what our country had done, but on this particular day i was feeling my own loneliness more than thinking about the atrocity the United States had committed on Japan. During my first year at the Colorado State College of Education in Greeley, i had been popular among the Independents and even among some of the young inexperienced Greeks (sorority girls) because i knew how to have fun — even without the boys. But the older more sophisticated Greeks apparently knew i didn't know how to have fun with the boys. I wasn't even rushed. Since my sister had been a sorority woman at Denver University, i felt slighted at first, though i soon realized the Independents were more my type. I hated dressing up, going to teas and being proper. So i had a lot of barbarian friends, but no one i was close to.

Since it was August, school would be starting again. Wondering what it would bring, i agreed to let my sister do a card reading. She was learning the art of fortune telling from my mother and wanted to try out her skills on me. Of course we were advised not to take it seriously, but we did. So did my mother. I had a strong premonition this was going to be a good reading. When she told me i was going to meet someone important in my life at school that fall, i was delighted it was a woman, signified by the Queen of Hearts.

Back at school, in September, my two roommates and i were apprehensive when our triple was changed into a quad, and an older woman of twenty-four (we were nineteen) was assigned to our room. She had even been teaching already! I was so apprehensive i didn't even recognize her as the Queen, although her light brown hair and hazel eyes denoted the complexion assigned to that card. Even though she was older and an experienced teacher, i sensed her discomfort at being the only one in the room who didn't know anyone. I offered to take her on a tour of the campus. When she told me she was majoring in Physical Education all my fears faded away. I was not a P.E. major, but i loved to ice-skate, play tennis, volleyball, and softball. She didn't do any of these things. She was into the physical fitness side of it. She was plenty fit herself, having been raised on a horse ranch in Wyoming. But she did want to learn to play tennis, so we got her a racket and i became her tutor.

On Saturdays we would go for long walks in the country, since both of us loved to listen to the rush of a creek, bird calls, crickets. But we always had to be back in time for her to go to confession in the late afternoon. She was a Catholic, and i discovered that she took her religion seriously.

Late in October i was attending a class in teaching elementary school music when I got the message that my father had died and that my uncle would be coming for me within the hour. Since my father had been ill with cancer for the past six months and had been in a coma for several weeks, i was not surprised, but the irreversible fact of death making me suddenly fatherless was still a shock. As i walked across the campus towards my dormitory i was strongly aware of the privilege of being alive. The grass seemed unbearably green against the intensely blue sky. The autumn leaves were brilliant reds and golds. I saw the Queen coaching a game of soccer in the field behind the gym. I wanted desperately to run over and tell her what had happened. Then i realized how much i wanted to enjoy this day with her. Did she mean more to me than my father? Since i could hardly interrupt her duties as a student teacher, i resolutely walked on by, hoping that at least she would see me and come home before i left so i could tell her of the turmoil of my thoughts and feelings. But that was not to be.

When i got back from the funeral, i was feeling guilty about not having loved my father as he wanted. He had always claimed i was his favorite, but i had hated him for saying that, because he used it to torment my sister. As I grew older he really wanted to be close, but i didn't. I not only saw through his ruse to get at my sister, i simply preferred my mother. The Queen understood this and held me while i wept, until my tears finally washed away the guilt.

Then she confided in me that the real reason she had come down to Colorado to finish college was to get away from the man who had jilted her the previous spring. It was my turn to hold her and assure her he wasn't worthy of her anyway.

When Christmas vacation came, she went home to Laramie and i to Denver. Never before in my life had i missed a person as i missed her that vacation. I could hardly wait until it was over so that i could tell her how i felt about her. I had never heard of homosexuals or queers, so i had no qualms about it. I remember the day vividly. The sky was brilliant from the setting sun. We were standing at our window in the dorm admiring it when i told her how much i loved her. She was somewhat surprised at first, but she did not resist my embrace nor refuse my kiss. Not long after that we were making love during the hours when our roommates were at class and we were free. Everything became beautiful as eros bloomed in me.

I loved the Queen's huge, floppy, soft breasts. None of the women in my family were so endowed. I named one of them Augusta and the other Abusta. I celebrated with them when she took off her very confining bras and they would plunge into my hands overflowing even my long fingers. Then i would gently nuzzle them with my nose, my whole face, and begin to kiss and caress them with my tongue, finally sucking the nipples which by then were more than ready. And the Queen would begin to moan and her back begin to arch. It seemed she had a direct current from her nipples to her vulva. She would grab me, thrusting against me. I would embrace her with one arm and with my free hand find her pulsing labia and enter her with one or two fingers. I did not know about the clitoris, but just from the shape of my hand, i am certain my thumb was rubbing her there as my fingers slid in and out, moved by her thrusting. I had also never heard of orgasm so was blessedly ignorant of the goal we were supposed to achieve. What became the high point for me was the ecstacy of peace, light and fulfillment i felt after the excitement of the lovemaking.

One day during our lovemaking, i suddenly had the desire to kiss her vulva. Heretofore, only my hands had pleasured in that wonderful moistness. Immediately i decided that that would be going too far! I had never heard of cunnilingus or going down on someone. But the thought stayed with me and fed my imagination. All the next day i thought about it, wondering how she would respond. Circumstances didn't permit us to be alone for several days. By the time we were together again, it was on a weekend when our roommates had both gone home. Such luxury! Hours could be had for our new pastime. Realizing that i would love to have her kiss me there, i took the plunge.

"Queenie," i said, "could i—un—could i (gulp)—would you— would you like for me to kiss you—there?" The pause before the answer seemed endless. Was she shocked? Revolted?

Finally a little voice replied, "I think i'd like it." I realized she also had had to consider if she would want to kiss me there in return. While i was most often the initiator of these things, i was no stone butch, and she was much into pleasuring me, too. I lifted the covers and went directly for her mons. I'm certain my heart was setting new records for fast beating. Then i found her moist labia and very shyly, very tentatively kissed them. Then i kissed them again with tenderness. And again with passion. Instantly her back arched and she pulled me up and clung to me while i brought her to climax with my fingers. It had been overpowering for both of us.

Perhaps it was too much so for her. A few days later she told me that what we were doing was a mortal sin. Having been raised a Christian Scientist, i was unfamiliar with the term. Sin was a product of mortal mind, but so was sickness. Nor did i wish to be cured of this by saying the Scientific Statement of Being. I hadn't read the definition of sex (if there was one) in the glossary of the *Science and Health With a Key to the Scriptures*. It was probably another product of mortal mind and, therefore, unreal. Besides i had quit going to Sunday school my junior year in high school.

The Queen, however, was finding it harder and harder to keep going back to confession, confessing *our* sin. Finally came the ultimatum. If we didn't stop she would have to ask to be assigned to another room. It was hard for me to believe that our lovemaking was wrong, but we were so close by then i decided the friendship was worth the celibacy. We still slept together when we had the chance, and hugged and kissed, but carefully left our genitals alone.

———

Excerpted from *That Strange Intimacy*, an autobiographical novel in search of a publisher.

Demons and Nightmares

Ní Aódagaín

She arrived
her car brimful of books and papers,
maps of the country she would travel across,
her heart full of hope, full of love, full of desire.

She arrived
we have a month together.
Then she will follow those maps to another place
where she will study those books and papers,
her heart full of hope, full of love, full of desire.

Or, will I kill that desire in her, that hope, that love?

It is entirely possible.
I have demons inside me
and nightmares.

INCEST IS A CHRONIC DISEASE

We lie together,
our mouths
open, wet circles
our tongues speaking with strength and beauty,
one to another,
exploring, meeting, sucking.
No words need pass between us.

She wants more
sucking
of breast,
more sucking
of clitoris,
more, more.
Her desire carries her
upward
tilt of head, neck open

to my
demons, the demons clench
my mind.
I retract
my lips, my body, my pleasure.
"It is enough. I am done," I think,
my head now in control.

Yet she wants more,
her face coming close to mine.
Suffocating, smothered,
I will be smothered.

I take her fingers from my cunt,
I turn from her
and burrow into myself.

INCEST IS A CHRONIC DISEASE

Another lover, another time
but not so long ago.
We were making love when
I heard their voices,
saw their faces;
my brothers live within me.
   "You are the property of the Family Egan.
   You do not have the right to love in this way.
   We alone hold the key to the chastity belt
   upon your orgasm.
   Stop! we say."
And I did.

INCEST IS A CHRONIC DISEASE

Again, this time, it returns
the voice, the feeling of being owned
of property rights, of brothers' power.

I am loving a womon.
I am pressing my body against her
our legs woven
one into the other
the lines of She/I diminishing
becoming less clear.

My finger within her
encircling, exploring
the innermost depths of her.
Our passion raw, uncontained
our bodies
arcs of strength and power
our mouths and tongues and fingers
the tools of our desire.

She pulls herself onto me
her body strong, large,
sinewed muscles of arm and leg
her tongue unbridled
looking, searching
for her mate
insistent, fast, unceasing.

She becomes he
the many he that laid upon me
whose lust overpowered reason,
whose minds ignored
my body's pleading to stop.
I do not want this anymore.
Enough. Stop.
I am suffocating. There is no breath.

I turn my head
the tongue searches for its mark
there is no respite
there is no escape.

INCEST IS A CHRONIC DISEASE

Finally I find my voice.
"Love, let me get up."
Immediately she withdraws her body
to the side of the bed.

I, shaken, reach for covers, to hide.
She finds me, encaved, pulls me to her.
The breath, halting
the pain in my chest, in my stomach
piercing
the sobs, only dry heaves.
The nightmares,

twenty years of nightmares
replay in my mind,
are unleashed by this loving.

She says, "I am sorry."

My reply, "You have done nothing wrong.
Hear me, you have done nothing wrong."

Wet tears fall upon my cheeks
the sobs now moistened by tears
hers/mine,
the lines diminishing.

"I love you," she says.
I look up at her.
The light upon her
encircles a face
transformed.

"You are beautiful," I say.

We hold each other.
Sleep comes over us.

LOVING IS THE WAY TO HEALING

Idyll: Four Days

Chrystos

We laughed so hard when we arrived at the tackiest motel room in the universe, replete with formica/chrome table & two rickety chairs, fake wood paneling & a spectacular view of the parking lot. In the coffin-sized bathroom, only one person could barely turn around. If you used the toilet, your knees were in the shower. If you bent to brush your teeth, your butt was in it. The kitchenette was of similar magnificent design. I needed to lose at least 35 pounds to fit in the narrow slot between the stove & sink — so I usually cooked & she washed up. I restrained myself from taking the marvelous sign on the back of the door: "DO NOT cook crabs in this room as it takes days to get the smell out."

However, as you'll see, the setting faded very quickly into the closeup of new lust/tentative love, where each curve is all that one sees & nothing is as good as the taste of her cunt rippling.

There was a color TV, newer than anything else by 20 years, which we attempted to use as camouflage for our sounds. Not successfully, for the following afternoon, we got dirty looks from the crabby young husband next door. I was afraid we'd be thrown out because we're both so loud when we come. I'd forgotten that no one wants to admit publicly what great sex we can have — they can't complain without severely jeopardizing the myth that "we're only lesbians because we can't get a man." Given how much everybody hates us — churches, governments, parents, schools, jobs, pizza takeouts, gas stations, banks — all the hate we have to shove off our backs everyday, we deserve hot sex. What a relief it is to be with a woman who is louder than I am, to never wonder did she come yet or still, that awful quivering silence. I love to hear yes, uh huh, harder, deeper, slower & finally cries from the shaking belly I recognize as they rush through my blood on out the top of my head.

Our dear tacky motel was located on the Oregon coast near Yachats, which is worth the seven hour drive from my place (also on a beach but one that is ringed like Malibu with houses, houses). You can walk or miles without hitting the barbed wire of Private Snobperty. The and was full of amazing swirling patterns from the oil spills, which were quite beautiful, though I'd give them up for clean beaches. On he way down, broom blazed yellow beside the roads, with pale green osebuds on the tips of all the evergreens. We drove under blue herons, hawks, eagles, an osprey & some dark geese very high up going north.

We met three months ago at a planning meeting for a National Lesbian Conference where we spoke intensely about politics. I don't remember a word now, as we glide through each other going to marches, speaking out, seeing political theatre which sounds like one of those earnest, sincere relationships with very little sex but I've never had sex so good. Just good. Sex where you spend all day in bed & never want to go back to work or talk to anyone else or put your clothes on. Sex that breathes. Sex that makes us wet in memory at roadside diners. She blushes when I talk about her pussy but she likes it. I know perfectly well that 'Pussy' is not feminist but "I love your vagina" just doesn't have the right ring. Pussy has sibilance like sex when you finally get enough or you could get enough if you didn't have to sleep, after 25 years of trying. A few times getting enough but with other incompatibilities that soon soured into go away. Have I finally figured out what I want with a woman & do I finally like myself enough to make sure I have it? We haven't fought since we met, we both consider this very odd, as veterans of long & short relationships in which we were always doing at least three things wrong & usually more; veterans of women who found our character flaws completely unacceptable but still wanted to go to bed with us, most likely so they could continue to tell us how angry they were about 'x' or 't'. We joked throughout the trip about what we'd fight about without ever managing to get angry about anything. I'm accustomed to having a nasty battle about one week or two into my 4 or 5 or 8 year liaisons. It is important that we're both sober. She's accustomed to girlfriends who don't think she's emotional enough or she's too emotional or wants to spend too much time together or needs too much distance. I make her laugh, which is good, as she's very serious. She actually enjoys & appreciates me which is balm after years of fear, resentment, envy, anger. She is supposed to be looking for a job, I'm supposed to be writing a play and a novel. Instead we drove down to spend days in inner & outer seas. I brought sexy nightgowns I never unpacked. We were in bed so much I didn't have to bring any clothes at all. We planned every night to get dressed to go out for a fancy romantic dinner at the place just two doors away but we never made it. She bought dessert there one night & brought it back to our bed full of crumbs & wet spots. Once we limped in around noon for breakfast, neglecting to take showers so that throughout the meal we chuckled as we lifted forks to mouths, smelling ourselves.

She is plump, round, with nipples who adore being sucked. She is dark-eyed searing eyes in which I am calmed & held still. She is dark-haired with silver spider's silk weaving her years, dark hairs on her belly swirling down, her divine greed. I reel in her smell, wind, seaweed, her gentleness, her butchness, the way she leans over me, her arms walls that shut out the noisy messy world & convince me that flesh sweet on flesh is all I care about. Her voice is deep, dark as she says hard words, shivery words, cunt squeezing words, hungry words, tasting me taste her.

Her mouth came looking for me nibbling my nape, her belly pressed into my ass as I turned the pancakes smiling. The next batch burned. My hand on her ass playing with her crack as she grunts, my tongue looking around for that magenta spot who goes ahhh whhoooo uh huh

Her thighs slapping my ears, I reach to catch her head falling off the edge. I'm wet to my knees taking her until I'm mindless need. She thinks she wants to stop "No baby" I say "Give me a little more I can feel it in you" & she does shouting over the feeble Motown tape

I smell my hands now when she has just left breathing in the light I've touched Pulling her back into me pushing into her my heart swirling my eyes weaving our names her skin that rises to meet me instead of drawing away & the restless hours before I'll have her again in my hands pulling off her shirt my teeth along her neck little bites my tongue in her ear as she shudders half pulls away because it feels too good

& the restless hours before I've her in my arms again pulling be hours & hours 21 long hours before my fingers are warm inside her where all the colors of life dance where she grips me so tightly my hands cramp I don't care & go on reaching into her pushing to our screams of joy wet glimmer of her lips tender rivulets roaring

In the evenings we went for walks when the tide was out, our eyes intently searching for agates, of which we found many.

Expansive Paradise

Katherine Davis

I've got a date. Time to start scheming. Being a not-so-closeted fan of those Dynasty and Dallas gals, I'm already planning which teddy I'll wear.

The blue undergarment glides over my head and around my waist. Abundant cleavage sneaks over the edge of the satin bodice. Snapping the crotch, I admire the smoothness of my thighs. Untold promise and pleasure await.

Hands on hips I scan my skirt collection. Between the white cotton and the denim, the gray rayon with the tapered waist draws me. In the bathroom I hang it next to the white shirt also intended for this evening's ball.

☆ ☆ ☆

We have been friends for several months now. And as friends, this is the first night we have spent together. She wraps her legs around my hips and holds my stomach. This is the first time I've spooned with anyone for over a year. It's the first time I've been in bed with a big gal like myself.

We are so sweet in our flannel nightgowns and bunny slippers. We haven't bought matching sets, I just happen to have an extra pair of everything. Fearful of deadly lesbian symbiosis syndrome, I clarify with her that this is a one night event and that I don't expect to do this tomorrow night or any night thereafter.

She answers by nodding her head against my back and sneaking one hand under my breast. "It's warm in here," she says. I fall asleep with her breath in my hair.

☆ ☆ ☆

My face in the mirror is pink and excited. The hotspots on my chest complement the teddy. Raising hands over my head, I admire the contrast of brown hair against satiny billows of my upper arms. Purple streaks of stretched skin look like lightning against ivory softness.

Katherine Davis

I hold my hands in front of my face. Five rings on my fingers and I fantasize I'm a wild rock and roll singer with a shock of red hair. As I powder my whole body, I'm dancing with Janet Jackson. Muguet lotion smells good and feels even better on my throat and hands. I put rose oil behind my ears, knees and, of course, deep between my breasts.

☆ ☆ ☆

We lay in separate beds in the same house. I can hear her giggle when the dog jumps onto her bed after I ask him to come sleep with me. I call him back, but all I get is the thump of his tail against the window frame. She tells me that I can come get him if I want him, and I remind her that we are sleeping apart because I don't want to jump into anything too quickly. And that I know that I want to do things with her that I am not ready for. I want to make my goal of one years's celibacy.

She tells me that she knows about that fear and that she also knows what I want. She tells me that she will have me on my terms someday. I ask her if she heard that line in a movie. She tells me that she is cold in her bed and don't I want to come visit her? I say no for the last time and fall asleep with my fingers on my nipple and my dreams in her bed.

We do not look at each other in the morning, only brush against each other on our way out the door. I tell my counselor about the night before. She asks me "where does she get those lines?" We laugh for different reasons.

☆ ☆ ☆

I pull the shirt over my arms and it hugs my hips and waist. As usual, I'm entertained by the little dot that marks my belly button. This generous roundness reminds me of baking bread, lazy lovemaking, hot baths and deep kisses.

The silk blouse sneaks into every crevice. It easily conforms to my ample breasts and my wide back. Three buttons undone down the front and a leather belt cinched at the waist drive me to distraction. Especially with the satin blue shadow under the third button.

Denim boots over black tights complete the look. Hands on my ass, I survey my finished self. I enjoy this solid width under my palms. I am at this moment unshakable and solid. I hold myself up.

☆ ☆ ☆

My back is to her. Once again in the same bed, once again on our sides. I fan my hair out on the pillow and she tells me not to tease her if I don't intend to come through on that promise. I tell her that I wasn't teasing her, even though I was. She runs her hand along my hip and into the curve of my waist. She presses her breast against my back and I feel her pelvis insistent against my ass. She asks me if I wouldn't like to know how it would feel to kiss her. I tell her I would very much like to know that, but I don't feel ready yet, and besides, I am too shy. She tells me I am sweet and before she turns over she lifts the hair off my neck and licks the nape.

I curl myself around her and my nipples harden against her back. I resist the urge to slide my hand into the neck of her nightgown and settle for rubbing her stomach instead. I graze my lips on her neck until I remember where this might lead. We fall asleep with my hands under the fold of her breast, my mouth against her ear.

☆ ☆ ☆

She knocks on the door and it's time to go. I can see the admiration in her eyes and she blushes when we hug. I can feel the heat through her flannel shirt. Shutting the door behind us, I admire the lavender ribbon in her hair.

☆ ☆ ☆

I have decided we can say we are officially dating. In my Virgo mind, the label legitimizes and encourages anything we may want to do with and to each other. We have returned from a movie and she has decided to spend the night.

I come to bed fresh from a scented bath. We are both surprised when I join her under the covers: she is wearing a lacy black satin body suit I have never seen, and I am wearing her favorite blue teddy.

We are awkward at first. Her debonair style has been replaced with the this-is-only-my-second-affair-blues and so I give up shyness and trade it in for the role of experienced lover.

I want to ease the pressure of this first night. I tell her that we don't have to do anything but like each other. This is as much for her as for me. She reaches for me and we hug and hold each other.

As things often go, it isn't long before we are stroking each other's backs, purring in the other's ear. I cannot stop myself from biting her neck as she takes my nipple between her fingers and rolls it back and forth. We moan together and I need more of her. Months of abstinence draw my mouth down upon her nipple like a magnet.

She arches her back in surprised delight and I hold her close to me. I look up for a moment and catch a glimpse of half-closed lids and open mouth. I leave my oral pleasure for a moment to lick the sweat off her lip, but I have to return quickly to that hardened knob my tongue loves to pursue.

I feel her silky motion under my thighs, and I nudge her legs apart with my own. For a moment we are suspended in anticipation.

I crawl on top of her and place my knee against her cunt. To my surprise she draws me up so that my breasts are in her face. She takes my nipple and teases, nibbles and tugs until I am sure she will eat my breast. That would not be a horrible way to go, I suppose.

My leg is slippery wet where she is riding, uninhibited, towards her satisfaction. I take my nipple from her mouth and move down to where I can kneel between her legs, spread open, for me.

I ask her what she wants and she moans in response. I tell her that I want her to tell me what she wants because I want to hear it. She spreads herself wider than I would have thought possible and I see what she wants. She asks me to put my fingers in and I will do that and more. I dip one finger into her waiting wetness and draw it in and out and around. I listen to what it says as it looks for the hooded jewel. She moans and I know what treasure I have found.

I crawl to the end of the bed and put both of her legs over my shoulders. Before I go down for a long time, I reach my hands up to play with both nipples.

She rises up for my mouth and I take her in. I am overwhelmed with the salty smell and taste of her. The honey wetness draws my hand and I plunge eager fingers in, deep and hard. My tongue nuzzles the heart of the rose and all it's petals. I meet the eager rise of her hips with deeper thrusts of my tongue and fingers.

She is pulling my hair, pulling me harder into her. I push back and cry with her as she passes from ecstasy and nearly swallows my fingers with her clenches. Howls of release fill the room. I keep licking and sucking until she pushes my head to the side.

We lay here together, my hand resting gently on her. She puts her arm around me and I put my nose up against her armpit. She takes my breast in her hand and tugs on me. I know that whatever happens here tonight will make the last year worth the waiting.

A Slow, Sweet Kind of Death

Rocky Gámez

When the telephone rang, Lucas was inside the closet in her bedroom, putting away cardboard boxes she had filled with most of her personal belongings. It was a hot summer day, and the clothes she was wearing were drenched with perspiration, but she had to finish packing the closet, although she felt wilted by the relentless heat. In a couple of days she would be leaving for California and she didn't want to be doing anything at the last moment. That evening she was going with some of her friends to Padre Island on the Texas coast, spend the Fourth of July weekend there, then come back to pick up her suitcase and leave for Los Angeles.

A week or so ago, she had received word from Nora that she was very sick in the hospital. She asked Lucas to come and be with her. She was afraid of the operation she was going to have and wanted Lucas to be there.

"Are you out of your mind?" Penny had said to Lucas when she told her she had made her plane reservation. "She left you for someone else six months ago! What the hell are you doing running up to her now?"

"I still love her," Lucas said. "Besides, she needs me now."

"You need *her* more than she needs you, *pendeja!*" Penny said in an accusatory tone of voice, and Lucas could not blame her friend for showing anger at her decision to leave the Valley.

Penny had been in very close contact with Lucas since her breakup with Nora and knew how much despair the separation was causing her. She shook her head slowly and tightened her lips to show her disapproval. "I know what sort of pain and anxiety you're going through, Lucas, but what I don't understand is why you're making yourself available to someone that betrayed you."

"I still love her, Penny."

"The hell you do! You're just obsessed because she dumped you. Your self-esteem has taken quite a beating, and you probably feel like a pile of shit right now. But Lucas, you're not such a dog that nobody else wants. Give yourself a chance, girl. Someone else will come along."

"She's sick, Penny," Lucas argued.

"So what? Are you a doctor or a nurse? All she wants is someone that will care for her for free while she's recuperating. Not just someone, Lucas, but a fool. And that's what you'll be if you go to her."

Lucas was thinking about the conversation she and Penny had had several days before, when she heard the telephone ringing. Fighting her way out of the suffocating dimness of the closet, Lucas reached the telephone in the living room, panting and praying that it would not be Penny canceling the trip to the beach at the last moment. She needed some sun, some fresh air, and quiet time alone on the beach to think about what she was going to do once she got to Los Angeles. She was not sure if Nora was still with the fellow she had run off with, because Lucas had been afraid to ask. All she knew was that the painful pounding inside her chest had become a gentle fluttering the minute she had recognized Nora's voice on the phone calling her from the hospital in California. And when she hung up, she had actually seen a light at the end of the dark tunnel she had been in for the last six months.

"May I speak to Lucas Daniel?" a low sultry voice said when Lucas picked up the phone. Her first thought at hearing the unfamiliar voice was that it was Salvador, a friend of hers who had a gift for mimicking female voices and a perverse passion for calling up Lucas with prank calls.

"Cut the crap, Sal," Lucas said into the receiver, "I don't have time to play games. I'm still stuffing my closet with a whole genealogy of junk. What do you want?"

"Lucas, this *is* you!" the voice exclaimed and then Lucas heard the rich deep laughter at the other end of the line.

However gifted her friend was about imitating female voices, Lucas thought that this peal of honest laughter was something he would never be able to reproduce. This was coming from the throat of a real woman.

Lucas apologized for her initial mistake. "I thought you were a friend of mine."

"Oh, but I am a friend of yours, Lucas. A ghost from your past."

"Really?" Lucas said.

"I won't take too much of your time, dear, since you sound like you were in the middle of some work. It'll only take a minute. This is Martha Montelongo, sister of Viola, a friend of yours from junior high. She asked me to give you a call while I'm in the Valley, give you her phone number in case you're ever in our neck of the woods."

Well, I'll be damned, Lucas thought to herself. Strange how things work in life. That morning when she had started to stash away her things in the closet, she had come upon an old yearbook from high school, and had sat for a long time riffling through the old yellowed pages, summoning ancient feelings for Viola she had long forgotten. Viola, a chunky teenager with long dark braids, had been Lucas' first crush, but nothing had ever come out of it except in Lucas' daydreams of the girl.

They had never had a chance to be alone, Lucas and Viola. Martha, the skinny little surly kid, had always insisted on tagging along with them wherever they went. Even when Lucas and Viola were studying, struggling with a difficult math problem, Martha was always present, breathing down Lucas' neck with that annoying sniffling she always had because of a chronic rhinitis condition.

"Martha, for God's sake, child, go blow your nose and don't come back until the end of the millennium!" Lucas would scream at her, but the girl would never move away from their presence.

She had made Lucas' teenage years miserable; and, as a result, Lucas had developed a strong aversion for her. She couldn't remember ever having hated another human being more than she did little Martha Montelongo.

Inside the yellowed yearbook Lucas found an old faded photograph she had long forgotten. It was a picture of the three of them taken at a roadside stand along the big highway. She and Viola were standing, flanking an old burro painted to look like a zebra. Martha was straddling the miserable-looking animal, a triumphant grin on her face. Lucas had wanted a picture of Viola and herself that she could frame and put up on the wall of her bedroom. When she told Martha that she didn't want her in it, the obnoxious child had thrown herself on the ground in an embarrassing temper tantrum and kicked her heels until the photographer, in a fit of impatience, had hoisted her atop the burro and snapped the picture despite Lucas' objections.

Lucas smiled at the memories the old sepia photograph had evoked in her mind and wondered curiously how life had turned out to be for the Montelongo girls.

The Montelongo family had moved to Houston in Viola's sophomore year in high school. At first, she and Viola had kept in touch with each other through long sorrowful letters in which they had expressed their loneliness for each other, promising undying friendship come hell or high water, but then, over the years, these letters had dwindled and by the time Lucas graduated from high school, they were only communicating through greeting cards on Christmases and each other's birthdays. The last time she had heard from Viola had been over ten years ago. She had received an invitation to her wedding. But by this time, that great love of Lucas' had been buried in a shoe box in her closet along with the other assortment of collected junk from her childhood years.

"What brings you back to this neck of the woods?" Lucas asked.

Martha said that she had come to San Juan to see her grandmother. "I wanted to see the old dear before I leave for Greece. I'm getting married next weekend and will be living in Athens until God-knows-when."

They talked for nearly an hour, summoning mostly the memories of their younger years, laughing at the animosity that had existed between the two. "Lucas, I would love to see you before I leave," Martha said at the closing of their conversation. "Could that be possible for you this weekend?"

She told her about her plans for the Fourth of July weekend and then added, "I'm flying to Los Angeles Monday." By this time Lucas was excited by the sound of Martha's voice on the phone. "Why don't you come with us?" She proposed, hoping that she would say yes even at that short notice. "Penny Morales is going too. You remember Penny? She still lives in your old barrio."

After a moment of hesitation, Martha said she would. "Grandma is probably tired of listening to me talk about my trip to Greece by now," she laughed good-naturedly.

Lucas could not understand the sudden exhilaration she had felt as soon as she hung up the phone. For six long agonizing months she had been in the clutches of a painful dark despair that had left her stripped of all the joy she had once felt for life. In that paralyzing gloom, after the breakup with Nora, life had ceased to have any meaning for her. She was a woman alone, unwanted, floating aimlessly without knowing how to connect again with the things that had once made her happy. She felt helpless against loneliness, that dreadful feeling of nothingness that Nora's rejection of her had left her with.

She knew that what she was doing by flying to Los Angeles to be with Nora during her convalescence was nothing but a pathetic case of groveling at the feet of someone who didn't love her anymore, but she couldn't help herself. Something had to fill that void in her broken heart. She felt obsessed with the idea that only Nora could do that for her.

☆ ☆ ☆

Riding with Penny to San Juan to pick up Martha, Lucas felt a sudden rush of excitement, something similar to what she had felt upon hearing Nora's voice on the phone calling her from California, but not as sweet. This feeling was not accompanied by dread or mixed feelings as to what would be awaiting her at the other end, but of the thrill of a pleasant discovery.

"Hope you two won't end up reviving old memories and end up drowning yourselves in the ocean," Penny kidded. "Shit, I remember how you used to torment that poor girl. Remember when we went to the river on that Easter Sunday and you draped that water snake on Martha's shoulders? That poor kid almost died of fright. If I remember correctly, Lucas, she peed in her pants."

Lucas laughed. "She had it coming to her. Lord, I wanted to lure Viola away from the group into the underbrush, but she kept on tagging along like she was my tail."

"Oh, Lucas, and remember when you wrapped that cow plop so nicely and gave it to her on her birthday? Now *that* was mean. Time came to open the presents and Martha says 'Mommy, mommy, I want to open the prettiest present first!' And, man, when you made a bee line for the door, I knew you had done something kinky."

"I hated that kid."

"Wonder how true it is about the thin line between love and hate?"

"Oh, stop it, Penny! My thing was for Viola not for Martha."

They were still laughing when they arrived at Grandma Montelongo's house. The old woman was sitting on the front porch, enthroned on the same old wicker rocker of yesteryears, reinforcing Lucas' sense of *deja vu*. It didn't seem that all those years had gone by as fast as they had.

Penny and Lucas got out of the car and went to greet the old woman. She told them that her granddaughter was inside the house, getting ready. "You might as well make yourselves comfortable," the grandmother said, good-naturedly. "My Martha takes days to get ready to go out."

Lucas and Penny leaned against the porch railing, glancing about at the old woman's exquisite flower garden. Lucas' yellow eyes panned the yard that teemed with native Valley plants. A swarm of voracious brown sparrows cavorted on the lantana bushes skirting the house, and the summer cicadas filled the warm air with their strident symphony.

For a moment, Lucas began to feel a painful nostalgia for what she would be leaving behind when she left the Valley, but she knew she had to leave it. For her own sanity she had to fill that void in her heart, that emptiness that only Nora could fill. She had been so in love with her when she had left.

The front door opened, interrupting Lucas' thoughts, and a tall willowy woman with dark hair cut a little above her shoulders came out smiling. She was wearing dark slacks and a yellow low cut blouse that exposed the soft brown contour of her shoulders. She came to Lucas with a mischievous twinkle in her large hazel eyes and threw her arms around her neck as though she had waited all those years for that precise moment.

Lucas had seen many beautiful women in her life, but Martha, that gangly obnoxious brat with the annoying sniffles, had to be the most beautiful of all. An unbelievable metamorphosis had taken place. She couldn't believe that this radiant woman with the fine chiseled features, bountiful breasts and feminine freshness was the same creature she had detested so long ago.

If someone had told her fifteen years ago that her heart would do flip flops at the sight of Martha Montelongo, Lucas thought that she would've died of hysterics. But here she was now, riding with her in the front seat of Penny's car on their way to the beach, unable to stop the accelerated beat of her heart pounding against her sternum with an excited wildness.

She could not stop looking at her now. She felt helpless, her head swimming within the whirlpool of her activated chemistry. Where was this creature six months ago when she was killing her ass for Nora? How far away was she when Lucas had committed herself to play the role of nursemaid to someone who didn't love her anymore? And why in hell didn't fate drop a hint or two before one reached the point of groveling and trampling on one's own self-worth? Jesus Christ! Wasn't life a precarious bitch?

When they got to the beach, the others were waiting for them in the parking lot. After they unloaded the trunks of the three cars and built an open fire against a sand dune, Martha slipped out of her dark slacks. The sun had already gone down and a gentle cool breeze was blowing from the Gulf. Lucas watched Martha and the others as they went into the warm water to meet the overlapping waves. She was a stunning figure in her yellow bikini, long dark hair and flawless skin. For a moment she felt jealous of the man that was to marry her and take her to Greece with him.

She picked herself up from the sand where she had been watching the group seated by the fire and went to stand by Penny's car, smoking a cigarette and sipping from a bottle of beer. She told herself that she was being stupid for allowing those feelings in herself, that she was setting herself up for another disappointment. Martha was straight, engaged to be married, and the only reason she had accompanied them to the beach was because she didn't have anything else to do for the weekend. She began to question her own feelings, that sudden rush of excitement that had come over her. When one was hungering for love it was tantamount to when one was hungering for food: any old tortilla would look like a real treat.

Martha was walking along the beach by herself, far away from the others. An army of noisy gulls glided over her head. In the moonlight, Lucas thought she looked almost surreal, like the whisper of a promise on its way to becoming a reality.

She ached to run to her, to be as close to her as she possibly could, to breathe the salty fragrance of the night with her. But she was afraid. There were still pieces of her heart that were clinging out of sheer desperation, refusing to fall. If she were rejected by Martha, there would be nothing left of her faith in love. No, she thought, she mustn't take that chance. She had to be strong for when she saw Nora again. One more heartbreak would reduce her to the pitiable creature she didn't want to become.

Penny came to her car to get a towel from the trunk. Lucas was leaning against it, smoking. "Are you creaming in your pants for Martha, Lucas?" she asked, smiling sheepishly at her.

Lucas flipped her cigarette away. "Don't be silly," she said. "Martha's straight."

"So was Nora, dear," she reminded Lucas with another grin and sailed down the sand dune to join the others who had gathered around the open fire to warm themselves.

Lucas lighted another cigarette, followed Penny down the dune, and took out another beer from the ice chest by the fire. Someone in the group began strumming a guitar, and Lucas knew instinctively that they were going to start singing the Mexican torch song that they always sang when someone in their circle of friends was suffering from a broken heart. She had been listening to the same song since her breakup with Nora. "You guys are going to sing the same old shit again," she said and walked away from the group, surprising herself at her annoyance.

As she walked away towards Martha, who stood at a long distance letting the foamy water lap at her feet, the lamenting words of the song followed her. This time neither the words nor the melody brought tears to her eyes. Something had distanced her from the pain the song had evoked in her before. And Lucas knew now what it was. She began to walk faster and when she got close to Martha, she stopped and sat on the sand to watch her.

After a while Martha came over to her and sat by her side. She was wet all over. Lucas could feel the silky texture of her skin as her bare arm brushed hers. "Lucas, are you going to spend all night drinking beer and sitting by the fire?" she asked, taking a hit off Lucas' cigarette. She blew a long cloud of smoke.

"You know, Lucas, I really didn't want to come tonight. For some reason, I was kind of nervous."

"Why?"

Martha shrugged her wet shoulders. "I don't know. Silly of me, I guess. Do you have another cigarette with you?"

Lucas took out the pack from the pocket of her parka and lighted one for her. She watched the moonlight casting sepia shadows on Martha's face and shoulders, then over her entire body as she stretched out on the sand, blowing smoke into the cool air.

"When I was little . . . don't laugh, you dreadful sonofabitch! . . . I used to have the biggest crush on you. Thought you were pretty hot shit. I always wanted to be with you but you were always so mean to me." She let her words wander into the salty darkness of the beach and after a long silence, she turned to Lucas. "Do you still hate me, Lucas?"

Lucas laughed at the tone of Martha's voice, it was that of the child she had mistreated so long ago. "Don't be silly!"

"When we moved to Houston, I cried, Lucas . . ." Martha began to laugh. "Did Viola ever tell you I had run away from home? Well, I did. I thought I could walk back to the Valley to come and live at your house with you. Dad caught up with me about half a mile away and spanked the holy hell out of me." She laughed again, that rich deep laugh Lucas had heard on the phone and liked earlier. Her glistening breasts heaved as she arched her back in uncontrollable laughter. Then she laid still, looking up at the swarm of twinkling stars.

Lucas bent over Martha and brought her lips to her breasts. She kissed them with much more gentleness than she had intended to, and feeling Martha's long fingers running through her hair, she began to kiss the soft arch of her throat until she reached her soft quivering lips, where her own lingered for a long time.

"Lucas, don't, please don't," Martha whispered in her ear. "I've never done this sort of thing with a woman before."

Lucas ignored her. Nora had said the same thing to her, too, and they had spent five wonderful years doing it until she had decided that gay life was not for her.

She undid Martha's bikini top and cupped her breasts with her sandy hands and kissed them with a flurry of feathery kisses. She could feel the fire beginning to rage inside of her, and soon, all the gentleness she had felt for Martha had turned into an all consuming desperate urge, raging through her head, her body, like a flaming storm.

Martha pushed her head back with both hands in a sudden movement that startled Lucas. "Lucas, if you're doing this to be the same sonofabitch you were to me when I was little, I swear to God, bitch, I'll kill you and feed you to the piranhas."

But Lucas was beyond words by now. Her hands were pulling down Martha's bikini bottoms. When she tossed the wet garment aside, she could feel Martha's hot breath on her ear saying, "God, oh my God!" She opened her legs and welcomed Lucas, giving of herself freely, unconstrained by what she might feel later about all this that was happening to her now.

In the distance they could hear the voices of the group singing the Spanish song, a lament about unrequited love, of dying little by little of a broken heart. But nothing mattered to them except themselves and the magic of that moment. "Lucas, don't stop! Please don't stop."

Lucas didn't dare to end that moment. She felt that she owed it to herself, to the beautiful woman lying underneath her. She had to prolong this puff of happiness in time and space for as long as she could. In that raging storm she felt inside of her, she could feel the love and loyalty she had once felt for Nora dying a slow, sweet kind of death. Rising out of the ashes of her despair and her loneliness was a brand new nestling, free to soar again on the wings of the affirmation she needed to love again.

They lay in the sand, their heads touching, their hands afraid to unlock from each other's grip.

"You know that in a few days I'll be flying to Greece, don't you, Lucas?" Martha said.

Lucas nodded without lifting her head. She was not going to try to fight this one and go into another helpless rage against herself. Martha had to do what she had to do. She knew this before she allowed herself to love her. In this there had been no betrayal and there was no way in this world that she would ever feel cheated, even if she never returned from her trip to Greece. She knew that if Martha had a change of mind later on, she would always know where to find her.

Lucas Daniel was not going to go anywhere for a long while. She knew that Nora would call her Monday when she failed to arrive at the hospital, but, for the moment, Lucas was not worried about what Nora would think of her now. She turned to Martha, caressing her inner thighs gently, as if it were the first time she was going to make love to her.

Cody Roberts

Willyce Kim

Seduction

"I desire you," said the voice trailing off into the warm evening air. "My heart sings whenever you walk by, and I can't keep my eyes off you, not for a second. I've strolled past your house and smelled the flowers in your front yard while hoping to catch a glimpse of you." Cody shook her head and stared across the Platte River. That's what she had meant to say. She had rehearsed those words for days. And now sitting there with Mary Lou Thomas, the senior prom queen, the hard-on of every young male at Lincoln High, the moment Cody had waited for rushed over her, drowning those thoughts like a flash flood in July.

"Mary Lou," Cody said, taking the most beautiful hand she had ever seen, "trust me. Nothing's wrong here, but so help me, I'm wild about you. I eat my breakfast in the morning, and I see your face swimming in my cereal bowl next to the berries and nuggets — and I want a second helping. I see you in the hallway at school and I want to climb those long white legs and . . . Jesus, it's bad at night. I can't sleep without . . . wanting you. I want to push my face into your hair and breathe all the flowers of the universe. I want you," choked the flustered Cody.

"And I, you," said the most beautiful voice in the world.

"Wait," said Cody, blinking wildly, "I must be brain dead."

"No," whispered Mary Lou Thomas, the senior prom queen. "This is Omaha. The North Star is overhead, and I'm going to take you for all the nights you've ever come alone in your bed."

Cody Roberts fell back into the tall grass of summer and pulled Mary Lou Thomas down beside her. "You smell like horses," she whispered excitedly.

"Well, come on, Cody," said Mary Lou slowly, unbuttoning her shirt, "let's ride, Cody, ride."

Armageddon

Jack Tucker was the first horse trainer in Nebraska to give Cody a mount. She was nineteen years old and weighed ninety-five pounds with her boots on. "Hell, to this day I don't know what made me give her the mount," he would say in later years. "I liked the way she galloped the horses in the morning, and I seen she had a way with them. She had good strong arms and a nice set of hands. She was spunky and always trying to chase down a mount, going from barn to barn introducing herself to the different trainers. She worked twice as hard as some of the boys. So I give her a shot, and I guess made a little history. She was the first girl jockey to ride at Ak-Sar-Ben. Hell, now it's nothing. We got three. But then, Cody Roberts was the first. She rode a big bay colt named Armageddon that day, and I'll never forget the stretch run. Cody had the horse on the rail and nailed the leader at the wire. In the winner's circle, she took off her cap and shook her hair down. The fans went wild and the press went crazy. It's a shame she left. She rode as good as any boy."

Grit

Cody Roberts with her dog Gypsy said goodbye to the state of Nebraska, said goodbye to Ak-Sar-Ben. Left her mother with her news clippings, her scrapbooks, and a soggy handkerchief; left Jack Tucker and his stable of horses; and left Frankie Tucker, daughter of Jack, in a stall, lying naked under a blanket of hay, to pursue her career at other tracks. Did she have the grit to go up against the other jockey colonies, especially the ones situated in the West? "Like the song says," she whispered in Frankie Tucker's ear, "I want to be the best in the West."

"Why, Cody," Frankie Tucker murmured, "you already arc."

"I'm talking about riding," Cody replied, clearing her throat.

"So am I," Frankie Tucker coyly answered.

"If your daddy only knew."

"I know what my daddy knows."

"And what's that?" asked Cody, panting as Frankie nibbled on her ear.

"That you have the softest hands since Shoemaker," Frankie Tucker whispered.

"Well," Cody said, gliding her hand over familiar terrain, "Daddy's always right."

Gumbo

Cody Roberts, on her migration west, stopped one evening at Louisiana Downs, a race track located east of Shreveport, to share a pot of gumbo with several of Jack Tucker's old stable hands. The evening ripened into several years. Cody stayed, a willing victim of Cajun cooking, reluctant to travel in mid-winter and itching to re-enter the winner's circle. She tossed her whip onto the track, encouraged by her old friends and a sweet-talking agent named Billy Bluestone.

Book

"I seen you ride in the Oaklawn Stakes one Memorial Day. You were on a filly named Khartoum, and you come out of the one hole, got shut off in the backstretch, took her wide at the top of the lane, and win the race going away. I'd never seen a girl jockey pump like that," said Billy Bluestone, shaking his head and smiling shyly at the ground.

"I remember that race," replied Cody. "That was my first stakes purse. Did you bet on me?"

"No," Billy said sheepishly. "I should have, but I wasn't going to bet no girl jockey in a stakes race. See what I know?"

"You know better now," said Cody, staring at Billy's brown eyes and the scar that creased the right side of his forehead.

"I do," laughed Billy, "and I'd like to prove to you how much I've learned, by being your book if you ride here at the Downs."

Cody scratched her head and looked over at the long lines of shed-rows and the horses walking to and from their stalls. If she stayed, she'd need an agent to work the backstretch for her. "Can you get me live mounts? I need good horses."

"I can get you the best," said Billy, sucking in his breath. "I know most of the local trainers, and it helps that you rode at Ak-Sar-Ben."

"How long you been in the business, Billy?"

"Ten years," said Billy, crossing his toes. "I booked my first mount at Bay Meadows in California."

"California," murmured Cody, tapping her chin thoughtfully. "I think your stock just tripled in value."

"Then," continued Billy, "I worked my way up the coast to Washington, stayed a while until I couldn't stand the rain any more, and ended up here."

"Well, partner," said Cody, extending her hand, "I have many plans, one is to win the Kentucky Derby. Another is to ride out west. And Billy," she called over her shoulder as she turned to walk away, "you can bet on that."

Way Out West

Cody Roberts lay with her arms around Frankie Tucker in the tiny sofa bed of her trailer. She was amazed at how easily they remembered what gave them their pleasure.

"A little lower and to the left," Cody had panted.

"Turn over, baby," Frankie Tucker had whispered urgently. Now, exhausted from their lovemaking, they rested in the afterglow.

Cody looked down at Frankie and thought how easy it would be for her to be swept away by the feelings that now overwhelmed her. She realized it would be a mistake to expect anything more than what had transpired. Frankie Tucker would, after all, return to Omaha and leave Cody holding a very limp bag.

Bermuda

Frankie Tucker made love to Cody Roberts all night. After the fifth session, Cody whispered faintly, "I don't think I can do this any more. I'm liable to pass out."

Frankie Tucker, lying dangerously between Cody's legs, grinned and repositioned herself on top of Cody's triangle. "Why, Cody Roberts, I never thought I'd live to hear you say that," she teased, kissing her thighs.

Cody Roberts looked down at Frankie and stroked her head. Frankie Tucker buried her face in Cody's groin and searched for the name tattooed on the fringes of her pubic bone. Lightly tracing her finger over the word, she called to Cody, "Say her name for me."

Cody tossed her head over the edge of the bed. Her hair touched the floor. "Bermuda," she whispered as Frankie moved lazily on top of her. "You're going down," said Cody slowly, "to drown in my Bermuda Triangle."

Excerpted from *Dead Heat*, a novel, published by Alyson Publications, Inc., 1988.

The Wet Night
(At A Bar XIV)

Lee Lynch

Sometimes, especially in spring, when Sally the bartender goes from Cafe Femmes into the tart mid-evening air, she is filled with a wanderlust. Tired, she'll meander home for what seems like hours through the perhaps wet streets of the city, hardly aware that her black felt crusher has begun to smell like damp wool and to drip as she pauses at corners, where she sways enchanted by the sharp reflection of red traffic lights in puddles, or by the sight of bright moist rows of strawberries, oranges, bananas and apples gleaming under the neon signs of small Korean groceries.

Most of the time, she feels full with this feast. Now and then, though, she aches for Liz to be by her side.

Blonde Sally opens Cafe Femmes in the morning. Shorter, dark-haired Liz closes it at night. They spend their day off together, and sleep every night touching through the dawn hours, forcing themselves awake to talk a few minutes as Liz comes to bed or Sally gets up. This schedule makes their time together delicious, even after all these years.

Tonight, Sally is drawn to a certain brownstone off West 4th St, as she would be to a secret lover. The owners of the building have preserved lilac bushes on tiny plots of ground to either side of its steps. During her worst fits of springtime roving, their phosphorescent glow lures Sally, especially in the rain, to a scent that bursts like a billion lavender explosions. She breathes them, and breathes them, until she is dizzy with oxygen and reels off into the night, longing to make love.

It's then that every woman on the street turns into a siren, and then that Sally walks among them like a connoisseur in a statue garden, drinking in every line.

That one with the wide splash of lipstick, blowzy, on the rakish man's arm. She wears an old-fashioned wide-brimmed hat, has hips Sally could spend a whole night kissing her way across. The woman's perfume rivals the lilacs for loudness, even makes Sally sneeze, but she stares after the couple, knowing the woman will laugh a full pleased laugh as they begin, later, in a creaking rented bed.

She loved that Liz laughed in bed, respectful of their lovemaking, but not serious.

She turns onto 6th Avenue, where there are more people, and her heart lurches after a quick-stepping fashion plate. Sally names her Nicole. Out of the trendy shopping bag on Nicole's arm peeps a baguette. She looks like she would not laugh during sex, and would allow into her life only lovers who did not disrupt her agenda. Even now she scurries to prepare a pretty, perfect plate for a midnight dinner: parsley just so, bread rounds toasted an exact tan, the apricot wine chosen for its color against her delicately patterned crystal. Nicole believes it's healthy to come once a day, hasn't the time to bother with more. Sally wants to stroke that prim sharp nose, pry the thin lips apart and find the lush tongue with her own. Wants just once to tear innumerable abandoned climaxes from the woman which would leave them both sobbing and laughing and glad.

She passes an awninged bar and considers returning to Cafe Femmes, where she could shadow Liz, spread her fingers around the bottom of her ass at opportune moments, steal kisses from a mouth sweet with the peppermints Liz uses to quell the taste of smoke.

The thought takes her back to the night, a month ago, when she'd woken from a seamy dream seething with desire. In it, a woman had been above her, open legs straddling Sally's face, pressing herself gently but rhythmically against Sally's pursed sticky lips and drumming tongue. Awake, but eyes still closed, Sally had exhaled a long breath. Her hand had discovered that Liz was home, sitting up in bed. She'd been reading *The Sunday News*. Not a promising sign.

"Hi, Babe," said Sally, hoping Liz would recognize in that endearment Sally's state. She was rubbing Liz's thigh with a finger.

"You're tickling," Liz said, squirming.

Sally turned onto her stomach. Her legs became entangled in the lower sheets.

"You're stealing the covers again, long tall Sal," said Liz, tugging them back across her lap.

Sally reached an arm across Liz's hips, accidentally on purpose disturbing the *News*.

"Sal!"

Finally, Liz gave her a sideways glance. Her eyes narrowed at the sight of the big wide-eyed grin Sally had prepared.

"Uh-oh," said Liz. "You're up to no good."

"You sure about that?" Sally asked, pressing herself against Liz's leg and rubbing avidly.

Liz had laughed then, filling the air with the smell of peppermint toothpaste. It had been a laugh so like that of the blowzy woman with the wide-brimmed hat and loud perfume that Sally's mind returns to Sixth Avenue now. She realizes that she's walked uptown two blocks without seeing a thing. The rain has stopped.

She wants more this night than going home and waiting for Liz. She turns east on 8th Street where the weekend crowds are teeming, and she joins their restless hunt for pleasure.

Sally wanders toward the sound of a woman singing. She is white and middle-aged, a sweet-faced street musician in peasant clothing, back-lit by an open bookshop. Two light-skinned adolescent boys back her up, one with short elegantly waved black hair and a fiddle, the other with a wild reddish Afro and a banjo. A hippie mother and her sons? The woman's long skirt sways as she sings, brushing the tops of bare feet. Over an embroidered blouse she wears a fringed leather vest dyed purple; her breasts push against it. Sally smells the spicy patchouli and is overwhelmed by the strength of it as she imagines her head between those breasts. She tosses money in the hat for the delight of looking.

"Any requests?" asks the singer.

Sally sorts through her skimpy knowledge of folk music. "*Mr. Tambourine Man?*" she asks, afraid the song had been too popular for a real folkie to deign to sing. But the woman, who has no Baez voice, but rather a full-throated almost bluesy style, throws herself into it as if this is her all-time favorite tune. Sally taps her feet and realizes how much she'd wanted to hear such a pied piper song tonight.

Once, when they'd still been new, just before they'd closed the deal on the bar, Liz had rented a car and they'd driven out of the city, without a destination, playing *Mr. Tambourine Man* and *Just Like a Woman* and *Lay Lady Lay* all the way to the end of Long Island, to Orient Point, where they'd waved goodby to a ferry load of people who were crossing to Connecticut. As much as she'd cherished the thought of marriage to Liz, she'd felt as if the Mr. Tambourine man in herself had been on that ferry. She smiles now, aware that he never left, and edges out of the crowd which swells around the singer. *Mr. Tambourine Man* follows Sally up the street.

It's about 9:30 now, long past dinner. At a deli she buys a package of apricot fruit leather in honor of the prim fashion plate and her pretty wine. She gnaws on the sour sheet of it until it seems sweet in her mouth. At Fifth Avenue, cloyed with the taste, she turns uptown to feed her other hungers.

A pack of punk girls who can't be over fifteen moves toward her. Their hair ranges from pink to turquoise, some of it spiked, some crew-cut, some frizzed. Like a cotton candy chorus line, they jangle their jewelry and pop their gum and walk to the rhythm of a raucous over-sized tape player. Underneath the racoon eyes, though, Sally sees the same tender flesh she'd first kissed, and loved, at their age. Behind the heavy pot odor, she knows there is still the fresh scent only young girls have, when their pores exhale dreams and sex is still a new kind of play. Her body recalls the heaviness of her own young need, knows her underpants will be damp the rest of the way home tonight, as they always were back then.

There is one teenager, at the very end of the cotton candy line, who meets her eyes. She's partly Asian, wears jeans and her hair is not as loud as the others'. The dyke, Sally thinks. She feels the girl's curiosity burn into her, feels the desire to take what Sally knows and learn it for herself, the where do I put my hand and when, and my tongue? Really, my tongue? And will you show me? Will you do it to me? Can I do it to you? Again? And again, please? Sally shivers at the thought of that slight frame, that new mouth on — not hers, but another fifteen year old who thinks she will die from the excitement.

Her legs feel tired. The fruit leather has been her only dinner. At the next corner she walks quickly back over to 6th and signals a taxi. The driver is a heavy black woman, who slouches against the side of the cab, one hand on the wheel, driving with a casualness Sally admires. She can see the woman's profile, and wonders about her. Can someone so in control of her vehicle be anything but a lesbian? She wishes the bullet proof barrier between them were open, so she could make small talk, probe with gay hints. Would the woman think she was trying to pick her up? If she did, would Sally follow through?

What would it be like, a one-night, a one-hour stand with a stranger? Sally had never done that. Would they go up to Sally's? Would the driver know a secret nook near the docks? Would she get in back with Sally? Would she take off Sally's wet jacket, then open her shirt? It was unthinkable that Sally could be the aggressor with this authoritative woman.

The driver, leaning against a door, would pull Sally's back against spongy breasts, would cradle her, talk to her in a strange baritone. She'd snake her hands around and maneuver Sally's pants down to her calves, push Sally's legs apart in order to explore her with those wide strong hands, twist Sally's head around to kiss her with a bold tongue, with a mouth that smelled of cigarettes. Sally would press against the driver's hand, her breath short, her desire for release desperate beyond any craving she normally had. She'd push against the heel of that hand with her clitoris while the fingers played around her opening. Self-conscious, she'd strain and strain. The driver, making wet sounds against her ear, would try to make her come despite the awkwardness of the back seat, despite Sally's feeling of helplessness at being so exposed, at being so passive. She'd expect to come suddenly, powerfully, at the thought of her unaccustomed passivity, abandoning her inhibitions to the majesty of the woman. But she wouldn't, too discomfited by strangeness. Finally, she'd lie weak against the driver, not knowing if she should apologize or just reciprocate. The muffled traffic sounds, the sight of dark warehouses, the fact of Liz, would seep back into her consciousness. She'd turn against the woman's breasts, really look at her for the first time, not just a hand, and not Liz, but another real person, a stranger.

And then? Then the woman would repulse Sally's advances, mutter about not wanting to 'get done,' drive her home and refuse a tip. Sally would be left standing on the curb, still admiring the big woman with the deft hands and the air of command.

They'd reached the theatre district. Sally rapped on the window to get out, half-afraid she'd revealed her thoughts in some way, perhaps through the fantasy meter ticking away on the dashboard. Embarrassed by the feeling of intimacy she had for this stranger, she tipped her too much. Sally stepped outside the cab and turned to the driver with a sheepish smile. Without a glance at her, the driver zoomed to the mouth of a theatre and picked up a man and a woman. Sally felt empty, abandoned, yet exhilarated. She'd had the pleasure of the encounter without the complications of reality. Liz need never know anything but Sally's spillover of passion.

Marquees blinked and blazed above her. She stood watching as the theatres emptied and the streets filled. Then the rain came down again. She wanted to laugh, to raise her mouth to the sky and catch the plummeting raindrops. A woman squealed. A man held a huge black umbrella before him and opened it mechanically with a whoosh. Now the umbrellas blossomed all up and down Broadway, slick and jouncing. Sally leapt over puddles in a private ballet, jubilant at having joined this huge party.

A lone older woman passed her in a belted trenchcoat and a rain hat slanted down over her eyes. All Sally could see of her face was a finely drawn mouth in faint lipstick under a long nose. The woman walked swiftly in sturdy black high-heels with hands in her slash pockets. Sally waited a while, then set off after her.

The rain muffled all sounds. The woman maneuvered through the crowds. She called no cab, but moved up Broadway with purpose. They passed restaurants and a few small markets. Sally's stomach grumbled, her hat dripped, her feet were sore and wet inside their running shoes, but the magnet of this woman, who must be sixty-five or even seventy, drew her past crosstown streets that were more devoid of traffic with every uptown block. Their only company was a parking garage attendant who stood in a gaping entranceway, arms folded, watching them go by. Sally nodded back at him.

She would tell Liz about this woman later. About the Amazon who stalked Broadway, luring younger women through the dangerous city.

Where would they end up if the Amazon had her way with Sally? On the very private balcony of a high rise on 5th Avenue, she decided. They would drink coffee the next morning in the Sunday sunlight. Young couples would stroll far beneath them with baby carriages. Roller skaters, joggers, looking very small, would enter the park. Widowers would snooze on the benches that line Fifth Avenue, and women would chatter to one another across them.

The woman in the trench coat would recline on a chaise lounge, her hair grey-white, her cheeks lined graphs around the jutting nose. Sally would reach to the woman's long robe and slide it open, letting her fingers rest on the grey hair between her legs. Their eyes would meet. The woman's lips, newly colored, would part. She'd let her legs fall open just enough. Sally would push into the nest, still damp from a shower they'd shared and her finger, barely touching, would roll back and forth, back and forth on the woman's stiff clitoris until her orgasm came, like another ray of warm sunlight, as quiet as the rain-washed Sunday city and the swarming park so far below.

But the woman in the trench coat didn't turn east on 59th as Sally had expected. Instead, she crossed as if going into the park. Sally drew the line there. She did not go into the park at night. She wanted to stop the woman, warn her. After all, hadn't they just—

No. Sally smiled to herself. They hadn't. The woman veered west then, not east, and Sally watched her enter the Plaza Hotel. Sally walked past the doors, craning her neck. An out-of-towner, she thought. Of course.

She was near home now, and, almost midnight, she knew Spot needed her walk, so she plunged through the rain the last few blocks, grabbed the Sunday papers and an hour later was in bed where she slept soundly until three A.M.

"Sal?"

Sally tried to wake up.

"I'm home, Sal," whispered Liz, and all of a sudden Sally felt at long last a naked woman's body covering her own.

She could smell city rain mixed with bar smoke on her lover's hair, and the peppermint toothpaste. Liz's skin felt tight from the night's tensions; her voice sounded a little raw from talking over the juke box. The windows were closed, but Sally could hear a squalling baby in the apartment across the courtyard. Liz's body met hers in all the important places, softness mixed with hard curves.

"Romantic, isn't it?" she asked.

"You mean the baby?" Liz laughed softly, rubbing her pubic hair against Sally's so it made the tiniest crinkly sound. Then she lay still against Sally, relaxing.

Sally feared that Liz would fall asleep. She ran her hands down the curves of Liz's back, rested her fingers around her waist, then began to stroke down Liz's ass over and over, spreading the cheeks a tiny bit each time she reached the bottom.

"Umm," said Liz.

Sally reached lower so that her spreading would pull Liz's lips slightly apart. "Do you like that?" she couldn't quite reach inside.

"All of it, Sal. I kept feeling your hands on me all night. I don't know what set me off."

"Whatever it was, I'll take it."

Liz opened her legs, tucked her feet around Sally's knees. This brought her higher. Sally slipped one finger in.

"Hhhh," gasped Liz. She pushed down on Sally's finger.

"I'd say you're ready, baby. Want to roll over?"

Liz shook her head against Sally's neck.

Sally moved her finger in circles, around and around inside the wet fleshy tent.

Liz kept gasping tiny gasps, jumped now and then. Her breathing quickened. Sally wondered if she was actually going to come, backwards like this. The thought excited her so much she lost her rhythm. Liz laughed, patient. Sally tried to catch the rhythm again while Liz pressed down on her finger even harder, then seemed to clasp it with herself, let go, clasp again. Sally held her breath for fear of breaking their rhythm again. She realized that the baby had stopped crying, that Liz's breathing was uneven, that there was absolutely no friction inside Liz now, just a pool her finger swam in, around and around and around and around.

"Hhhhhhhh," breathed Liz in a quiet exhalation. Her tent yawned hugely, then folded down tight. "Hhhhhh. Sal. Oh god, Sal. Oh."

She held Liz to her, felt their two hearts thump, kissed the side of her forehead. "I love you."

There was silence for a few moments. Sally wondered what her other lovers were doing and smiled into the dark. Had that cab driver quit for the night? Did the prim woman have her orgasm yet? The street musician had taken her sons to a coffee house where they were jamming still. The theater-goer, had she put her sturdy heels outside her door for shining? She felt a pang when she thought of the punk baby-dyke. She hoped the kid had a girlfriend who was sleeping over that very night. Stealthily they were exploring each other's bodies, making sensations of which they'd never dreamed. She began to stroke Liz again.

"That was very nice, Sal."

"Was it, babe?"

"I'd try it on you, but you're too long."

"Maybe you can come up with something else."

"Think so?" asked Liz, leaning over Sally, grinning eyes and teeth faintly visible in the dark.

"You always have before." But Sally was sleepy now, didn't know if she had the steam it would take. She told this to Liz and let her eyes close, snuggled in, content with intimacy.

She wasn't sure, a moment later, if she'd dropped off, and woken again, or if she was dreaming. Had Liz put Bob Dylan on the stereo? How could she know about Mr. Tambourine Man tonight? Had that really been a fantasy meter in the cab? She never opened her eyes to ask, though, because it felt too good, what Liz — was it Liz? — was doing, with her mouth, down there.

Sally hugged Liz's head with her thighs to tell her she was awake. Liz was blowing on her, with a warm breath that felt like a Sunday breeze. Just holding her open and blowing up, then down, then up again. Sally began to throb, glad it was Liz's full lips so close to her, not Nicole's thin prim mouth, nor the finely drawn lips of the out-of-towner.

Then Liz did something she'd never done before. She thrust her tongue inside Sally, suddenly, and as suddenly, replaced it with her fingers.

"Liz," she said from the shock of it.

"What is it, Sal. Again?"

Sally wondered if the baby-dyke had discovered this trick yet. "Oooph," she breathed as Liz tongued her repeatedly. "That's an amazing feeling."

"Kind of rough on the tongue muscles, though," Liz said with a laugh.

That laugh. Like the first woman, who had probably long since let her creaking bed go silent. She could see the motion of Liz's head in the dark, moving it back and forth to rest her tongue muscles. Sally felt her own wet parts stretch up. Then Liz's head dropped. Obviously, her tongue had recovered. It moved in just the right ways on just the right places and Sally, out of steam or not, could only follow the feel of Liz's tongue and the hot waves of tension that shook her body.

Her breath became as short as Liz's had been. She knew she was flowing like a fountain. Her body felt like — she wanted to say like it had come home, but how could home be this exciting? Maybe it was the spring, the lilacs, the rain, the neon lights, the women on the street and her long spring ramble, maybe it was all of that she was feeling as Liz — Sally gripping her shoulders for dear life, a long loud cry at last rolling from her — as Liz brought her home.

Guaranteed a Story

Jo Whitehorse Cochran

Loaded up with an easel, paint box, palate, camp stool, lunch box, dog rope, files, binoculars and camera, Celeste RedBird and Jenny Vaughn teetered down the stairs. At the bottom, Jenny faced the cabin with its weather-peeled paint and decaying shake roof and yelled, "Emma, Emma! We are here! It's Jenny!"

No response.

She had neglected to see if the car was at the top of the drive. However, a giant Siamese cat appeared at the window when Jenny called for Emma. Must be her cat.

Jenny and Celeste set about digging into paint and doing office work. Artemis, the dog, had just settled down in the high grass when a car rolled up at the top of the hill. Jenny and Celeste held each other's gaze as the door shut.

A woman with a box filled with groceries methodically came down the stairs, as if this was part of a ritual, done in a precise repetition. Celeste admired her tenacity and the glints of grey hair. She took a quick stock on Emma — Lee Jeans, a bright red IZOD shirt, collar-up over a chamois shirt (a beautiful doe skin color as if the woman were wrapped in a soft doe hide), and sensible shoes, gym teacher shoes.

Celeste's mouth wound into a wry smile. No doubt a member of the club. Celeste was a bit wondrous at what a lesbian was doing in this last bastion of timber money, pomp, and ol' boy country. Oh well, she was down the stairs, looking at them and smiling.

Emma was the first to begin the conversation. "Well, I'm glad you came."

"We brought you some freezer jam, raspberry, I hope it's still okay," Jenny replied, as if they were old friends.

Emma smiled, "Come on in."

Jenny, always the artist first, motioned to Celeste with her head. "I've got to stay and paint, but Celeste can help."

Celeste followed her cue.

Emma balanced the box of groceries on one knee and fished for the key in her pocket. Soon the door was open and they were blissfully in. The large Siamese dropped from the window to pad by Celeste's feet. "Oh, that is Kwan Yen. She is quite a presence and my best caretaker," Emma said. Lesbians and cats were inextricably linked in Celeste's mind.

"Jenny tell you how we met?" Emma asked.

"Yeah, it happens on her job that she meets a lot of people, but not often someone that knows about Gertrude Stein."

"Well, I'm a professor of Literature, the ex-patriots, at the University of Montana at Missoula."

"Oh, my people are from the Rosebud Reservation and Rohan Reservation." Celeste smiled thinking this is a woman who knows of the wide expanses of the prairie.

"You must be Sioux."

"Yes."

Emma directed her attention to stowing the groceries away. "I'm here working on a biography of Winifred Bryher, Hilda Doolittle's companion of forty years."

"Yes. We studied them in a Women's Literature Course at the University."

"Who did you study?"

"Gertrude Stien, Djuna Barnes, Radcliffe Hall, H.D., Bryher, Audre Lorde, Adrienne Rich. It is uncanny how there is such a recognized gap between generations."

"My partner Evelyn used to say the same thing."

"Your partner?"

"Evelyn and I were together for thirty-two years."

"Then you know about Jenny and me?"

"Well, I guessed about your Jenny. You seem good together. Would you like some coffee?"

"Sure, but don't bother for me. You must have work to do."

"No trouble. I've not had anyone to talk with or do for in two months."

Celeste sat on the couch next to Kwan Yen and offered a hand for an introductory sniff. Kwan Yen rubbed her nose wetly along it and purred. She glanced down at the coffee table. Another manuscript, separate from Bryher's biography, was taking form. Celeste felt guilty, but let her eyes scan the pages. Her cheeks began to flush as she read the two pages left open for proofing before her. Emma was writing erotica. She almost laughed. Leave it to Jenny to find the lady professor lesbian closet erotica writer. She wondered how Emma could publish this, how could she read it aloud in public, how? Emma didn't really appear the part. She was the intellectual sort from a small town, bookish around the edges. Celeste caught herself stereotyping. This day was proving interesting.

Celeste kept trying not to read the pages spread before her, but her eyes were fastened on the words ". . . her fingers curled inside her lover's vagina, slowly reaching the pulse of her, then drawing back as her lover's hips arched to the rhythm of penetration, the throbbing welling inside of them . . ." Celeste blushed, heat rising in her cheeks. She heard Emma rattle the cups in the kitchen.

☆   ☆   ☆

Jenny looked up from her canvas. She had the color and shadow down. The rest of the painting she had committed to memory. She glanced back at the house then stood and began gathering her tools. Artemis came nosing up, as if she'd been waiting for this.

"Yeah, I'm done for the day, Art. The light's almost gone and we're both hungry. Go get Celeste." Artemis dashed off to Emma's door and barked.

☆   ☆   ☆

Celeste looked up from reading the Bryher biography. "I bet Jenny is finished and hungry."

"You can let the dog in, Kwan Yen won't mind. I hope you two will stay to dinner."

"That would be wonderful, Emma. Thanks." Celeste opened the door and Artemis dog wagged in. "Jenny, Emma has asked us to supper."

"Great. The canvas needs to dry a little. And I missed lunch. Did you call me?"

Celeste smiled, rolled her eyes and said, "As always, honey." They laughed. She helped Jenny square everything away.

Jenny whispered, "How did it go?"

"Great! Emma is amazing — her lover, Evelyn, died last year. She's writing a biography of Bryher that is right on target. And another manuscript that is surprising." Celeste lowered her voice. "Jenny, it's erotica. I almost didn't believe it."

Jenny chuckled. "Emma might be a hot old dyke. Just gaze into her great green eyes. And that shock of grey. Well, c'mon Celeste, not everyone's like you, a shy girl."

"Look who is talking." Celeste shot back.

"That's why we're so perfect together."

Celeste had teased Jenny about her painting — so few works of women's bodies, why not a few nudes? Then they both decided that they'd be embarrassed if anyone thought the nudes were Celeste. This strange feeling overcame them if anyone in the women's community might think their bodies beautiful, erotic, desireable; or worse yet, not.

☆ ☆ ☆

Jenny stretched lazily on the sofa. "Emma, that was marvelous, the chili and the cornbread." Celeste curled up next to Jenny with Kwan Yen uprooted and headed for Emma's lap. "So what's this that Celeste says about you writing erotica?"

Celeste gave her a wicked glare. "Jenny! Emma didn't show it to me. I'm sorry Emma, I snooped." The manuscript had been cleared from the table hours ago.

"It's alright Celeste. I told you I was coming out. And I'm too old to be embarrassed or shy, and too proud to have made love to the same woman for thirty-two years to hide anymore."

"Well, why did you choose erotica?" Jenny kept in there.

"Although we were not out in Missoula, Evelyn and I were proud of our relationship. In the late seventies some of my younger students introduced me to lesbian feminist authors. I became involved in Women's Studies and Evelyn and I began to attend conferences. We found the voice, the radicalism that our natures craved. We began reading novels and looking for lesbian erotica. We found good sizzling works but we never found erotica about lesbians in couples. So, at forty-two, I began writing erotic poems, short stories and letters for us. The pages that Celeste saw were some of my first attempts to take those eleven years of work and format them into a book. I have a few ideas, but it's not pulling together like I want it to. Celeste is the first woman besides Evelyn and myself who has read any of it. I have books and books, all as handwritten manuscripts. All unedited." Emma looked at them. "Maybe you and Celeste could help. I have two binders arranged in a way that I think they might work as books. If you could read them, I'd like your opinions and comments. What do you think?"

Jenny smiled, "Sure, it would be great!"

Celeste laughed. "If I can keep from continually blushing, I would love to."

☆ ☆ ☆

On the drive home there were shy glances between them, little brushes of hands on each other's knees and thighs. They wove the unspoken language of a couple courting each other.

As they brought the last load of gear in, Jenny grabbed the binder, looked Celeste right in the eye and said, "It's Saturday. We can be up late. We'll start tonight."

Celeste, in a low voice, said, "Sure." Her mind raced on a bit. For all of her love and lust of women's bodies, scents, smells, touches, it was something else to read erotica in bed and have her own body exposed. This was silly. She had been lovers with Jenny for over five years — and yet they were still shy. This was a new kind of intimacy, a place where Celeste's reserve could not hide her. This was a prelude, perhaps foreplay unfamiliar to her, a singing of women's bodies. And it didn't seem to humble, disturb or daunt Jenny. Ah, Jenny. How like her.

☆　☆　☆

Jenny waited, curled under flannel sheets. With each shift of her weight the old bent frame bed creaked a comforting song as she nestled in. Celeste was taking her time in the bathroom. Jenny was just as pleased. She had lit candles and left the corner lamp burning low. Erotica must be read in the proper atmosphere. She chuckled at herself and shifted again.

They had read erotica before to each other, but never about someone they knew or in this provocative setting. She could feel Celeste throwing her head up like a deer hearing something stir deep in the underbrush. Jenny felt like the slender naked wood nymph of myth forming from the morning mist, drifting, glazed with the dew, shimmering in the early sun, appearing to befriend the doe.

She often experienced and mediated on Celeste with that image, a powerful, wily doe whose flank flinched a bit at the first touch, the pulse of wildness alive at the skin's surface. Any second she would bolt, the lush green understory of the forest closing behind her, claiming her as the mother's own. She had never spoken to Celeste about any of this. It seemed like a mixture of their cultural mythic consciousness. Maybe one day she would paint it.

☆　☆　☆

Celeste towelled off her back and butt, pressing her fingers through the towel to feel still-firm muscles. At the turning of thirty the body began to question itself, learning its age and remembering the easy tone of earlier days. She had been rock hard in her youth, riding horses, climbing trees, playing softball, basketball, volleyball. Her body always delighted in any physical challenge. Her body and spirit sang in the uncloaking of her sensuous self in the lavish lovemaking of those years from sixteen to her early twenties.

And then only with Jenny over these last five years. She smiled wickedly, just with Jenny who was waiting in bed. Over the past months it had been hard for her to let go of her literal, vigilant, serious mind. Somehow the sensuous and sexual, the erotic, could not boil up through this heavy layer of seriousness. Drawing in through her own body, she had re-lit the spark. She ran the towel across her brown belly, felt a little softness and smiled as she grew into this woman, the hard edges of her youth were letting go to a powerful womanly grace.

☆ ☆ ☆

Celeste slid between the sheets. Jenny was propped up on pillows, knees drawn up, becoming a lap for the binder. She smiled with that dark gleam in her eyes. "Lets go to work."

The first few pages were a short story taking place on the open prairie and grasslands of Montana. Two women on horseback, lovers, were off the beaten path, out for a picnic lunch. It was Emma and Evelyn. [Because it was women, there was the connection. It could be them also.] As Emma and Evelyn lay in the tall grass watching faint clouds dance in the summer sky, Evelyn lazily turned, gazed into Emma's eyes and began unbuttoning her shirt. Celeste slipped her hand onto Jenny's belly, slid it down to rest on the crest of her mons — delicately ruffing Jenny's pubic hair with her fingertips.

Evelyn bent to cup Emma's breast, gently lifting it from the white lace of her brassiere. Celeste bent and pressed her lips lightly to Jenny's belly at the rise of her hip. "Celeste, are you listening?" Jenny asked.

"Uh-huh." Celeste paused, looked dreamily up into Jenny's eyes. "Keep reading. I'm beginning to be inspired."

"We're supposed to be giving our opinion . . ."

Celeste nipped Jenny's thigh with her teeth. "I am, dear. I am. Keep reading."

Evelyn sank deeply into a kiss with Emma. Her hand smoothing Emma's breast, her fingers rimming the aureole and then teasing the nipple erect. Emma rose into her touch . . .

Celeste descended beneath the comforter. Jenny paused mid-sentence, began again as Celeste squeezed her inner thigh. It was difficult to continue, to concentrate on the words before her, as Celeste caressed her thigh with kisses, ran the tip of her tongue along her leg to her labia. Jenny ran words together.

Softly Celeste toned, "Slower, I don't want to miss anything."

She slid her hands under Jenny's butt, cupping her firm ass and lifting slightly with her fingertips where they fit into the small of Jenny's back, in the downy hair. Before kissing Jenny's labia, Celeste inhaled the sweet scent of her lover, like the succulent fruit of summer. It was a whispered blessing, inside her, inside Jenny. Celeste graced the moment, just before tasting the center of that magnificent pome.

Celeste glided her tongue between the folds of Jenny's labia, bringing forth the hooded pearl. Tongue and lips closing, dancing with the erect joy of her clitoris, pressing. And Jenny answering back, her feet anchored flat to the bed, carrying her forward to Celeste's long slow kiss.

Jenny let the binder slip away, pages yet to be read. She eased her hands down onto Celeste's shoulders, then brought one hand up to her mons, spreading the folds of her labia wider for her lover.

Celeste drew a hand out and carefully traced round the opening of her vulva. Jenny gripped her shoulder slightly in assent — yes, continue, inside. Through the moist hollow, Celeste guided her fingers, finding the rippled curve slightly under the pubic bone.

Jenny twined her fingers in the thickness of Celeste's hair. In the waved rhythm they spiralled in their sensations, tensions calling — Celeste's strong hand continuing, quickening, penetrating. Jenny, taut, rose to her, pushing a low moan from her core as they entered the prelude to orgasm.

Coupled in this music, Celeste thrummed Jenny's clitoris with her tongue, bringing her full, hard, jewel between her lips. They rode the pulsing. Jenny pressed Celeste's head in her thighs, bracing her face. The deep welling answered, Jenny's volcano of orgasmic sound, delight, rushing them.

Celeste gently withdrew her kiss and rested her cheek on Jenny's belly, moving her fingers into the cavern of Jenny's calling.

This was the moment. Jenny dug her fingers into the sheets. Celeste stiffened in the staccato pleasure of her lover's orgasms as they built each upon the other until, in a fierce drawing forth, Jenny climaxed and lay out of breath with delight wafting over her body.

They lay entwined, Celeste's head on Jenny's belly, Jenny's hands placed on the flat of her back. The energy moved between them — warm, the colored hues, greens and lavender.

For unmeasured moments they bathed in the energy and Jenny's after-tremors. Finally, Celeste whispered, "So this is some opinion of Emma's erotica." The laughter was releasing, splendid.

Jenny drew Celeste onto her, fiercely held her gaze, and said, "I'm not through with you yet, Redbird. The night is still ours."

The blaze of Jenny's intent caught Celeste off guard. She rolled away onto her stomach.

"Don't think you'll escape me — you can't play shy now." Jenny began with the back of Celeste's knees, kissing, nibbling, working her way up to her bottom where she stroked Celeste with her breasts, her hard nipples, imagining the sensuous delight as she did the same to the length of her back.

"Come on, I know you're with me." Celeste buried her face in the pillow. Jenny smoothed her breasts and hands back down Celeste's length to her bottom. Again she teased her with erect nipples, feeling her clitoris tingle as Celeste moved with her this time, silently. Celeste arched her hips. Jenny grasped at the top of her hipbones, pulling her up to her knees. She slid one hand between her legs and into the wetness of Celeste's vagina, fingers moving round and deep, then the whole of her hand, penetrating, as she felt the throbbing rise. Jenny slid her thumb onto Celeste's clitoris, now hard like a perfectly smooth pebble, and rubbed with the motion of her whole hand.

Celeste's body tightened, hands gripping the pillow as she arched into a shaking orgasm. Then she eased flat to her stomach as Jenny moved aside.

Celeste turned over onto her back. "Come here?" she asked, out of breath. "On top of me."

Jenny eased herself onto Celeste, pausing slightly as Celeste reached down and deftly parted their labia, revealing their clitorises. Then gliding both of them together, arching, engorged. They began in unison a slow melding, humping. Jenny pushing in, Celeste meeting her and riding through on the uptake.

Their bodies glistened with sweat as Jenny rose on her hands, her breasts swaying with the motion, seeming fuller to Celeste. Celeste reached up, took both of them in her hands, gently rubbed the nipples to erectness between her fingers. Then, bringing Jenny slightly forward, took the nipples in her mouth and sucked as they came together.

Exhausted and radiating, they lay curled together. "We have a lot to tell Emma." Jenny said.

Celeste smiled. "We have twenty-seven more years. We'll have to keep reading to find out if sex gets better and better."

Sheet Dancing

Corbett

The dinner of flirtation and innuendo was soon over. As I walked into the living room, Vanetta put her wheelchair up close to my crutches. She extended her right hand from the wheelchair arm, tucked her spastic fingers into my belt, and began to pull me towards her, calling, "Come to me."

That was all I needed. Pulling myself upright, I began to unbutton my blouse. I had dressed in pale silk for the occasion. Soft silk outer garments, with no undergarments. I knew I'd be wet before too long. I slowly opened my blouse while Vanetta drank in my luminous skin. My breasts gradually began to consume the entire landscape before her eyes, completely covering the breadth of my chest. They were as large as cantaloupes, but bursting with the fullness of vine-ripened grapes, oozing with juice.

Vanetta leaned forward, calling to the offered lusciousness, drawing the fruit into her warm and waiting mouth. Maria quietly moved behind Vanetta's chair. Her fingers traced Vanetta's sinewy back up and over her shoulders.

As Maria rolled her hands down towards the waiting breasts, Vanetta turned to face her. Maria felt Vanetta's hot breath on her face, smelled the primal scent of arousal. Reaching the upturned breasts, Maria found soft, hand sized breasts resting on the upper front edge of Vanetta's corset. Her toffee colored breasts were pushed up and together, two soft globes, nipples tightening under Maria's drumming fingers.

As Vanetta's nipples became harder, she grew more excited. My nipple was in her mouth, my breast covering her face. Now her own nipples were taut from Maria's stroking.

Letting my breast slide from her lips, she was drawn up to Maria, hungering for her mouth. Maria slowly leaned down, dancing her lips over Vanetta's soft black curls, tangoing across her forehead and finally waltzing on her lips. Vanetta, breathing rapidly, sucked in Maria's tongue.

Vanetta's fingers found my silk covered crotch and began strumming in accompaniment to her lip's dance. Maria's tongue slid and shimmied across Vanetta's sensitive neck. As I reached down to play with her breasts, Vanetta twitched, moaned and screamed.

When she caught her breath, Vanetta said, "I want some more of this . . ." We moved into the bedroom.

☆ ☆ ☆

Maria, the ever sensuous blind girl, said, "I want to undress you both." She began with me. I sat on the bottom edge of the bed, twisting slightly to face Vanetta. Maria took my crutches, put them into the corner, smiled, and said, "Your legs will be rubber soon, and these crutches won't help you at all."

Maria slipped my soft silk blouse from my shoulders, sliding her hands over my strong arms, built by hours of wheelchair basketball. As she pulled the shirt over my wrists, she commented, "So strong. Been doing endurance training? You'll need it tonight."

She moved her hands up my sides to my large breasts. She put her face into my breasts, kissing each hello, saying, "I've always thought these could never be appreciated by only two hands and one mouth. But with four hands and two mouths, who knows?"

Her fingers danced down towards my navel. "Ah, the Pearl," she sighed. She had personally named my perfectly rounded, pearl-shaped belly. She said it was a gift from the goddess: no matter how skinny I became, I would always carry this soft place for resting her head.

She pulled my silk pants over my full hips, down to my atrophied legs and my 'baby foot.' She loved how this foot is just the right size to fit into certain private places on special occasions.

As Maria was undressing me, Vanetta was holding me in her eyes. She had slid from her wheelchair to the side of the bed. She raised the head of the bed, so she was sitting up with her legs out in front of her. "A bed that moves," said Maria, "so many interesting possibilities."

Maria went around and stood between the wheelchair and the bed. I climbed into bed. Maria lifted Vanetta's shirt off, touching her rich brown arms. They were soft, deep, smooth. Like a woman's skin at both infancy and very old age. In Vanetta, it held a hidden tenderness that she had carried throughout her life.

When Maria began to unfasten the encasing corset, Vanetta protested, "I always do that myself." But Maria just smiled and began to finger the closures.

"Wait," I said, "I want a taste."

The corset held Vanetta's breasts as if on a shelf. Her coffee colored nipples covered half of her breast. With my tongue leading the charge, I circled the smooth dunes. Soon the dunes began to grow; not just harden, but grow, into Himalayan mountains with small sharp peaks and deep furrowed crevices. As I tongued them, my saliva ran down in rivulets.

☆   ☆   ☆

Maria became impatient. She wanted to release the soft yielding flesh. She yearned for the corsets of yore with satin and whalebone and ribbon. But modern fabrics are canvas and closures are Velcro, so she improvised. Singing the Gypsy Rose Lee Stripper tune, she pulled the closures open in rhythm: da-da-de-dum-RIP da-da-de-dum-RIP.

Beneath the corset was a cotton, spaghetti-strapped chemise. Vanetta's sweat had molded the chemise to her skin. I remembered this ritual from my own childhood, the precious sensation of the unleashing of the flesh. The orgasmic experience of removing the cotton garment.

Looking into Vanetta's eyes, I reached out and grasped the bottom of her chemise, slowly pulling it up and away from her torso. She sighed with deep relief. Maria began to gently finger the fresh skin indentations, fascinated by the braille hieroglyphics. Her fingers darted across the symbols, seeming to decipher the information before it faded.

Vanetta and I were unconcerned with Maria's fascination. We knew that tomorrow there would be new symbols to decipher. We had held onto each other's gaze. A moment never before shared, totally knowing the other's experience, bonding our deepest selves.

"No one's ever liked this part of me," she said.

"There are more surprises to come," I promised her.

☆   ☆   ☆

Vanetta slid to the middle of the bed. Maria and I gently pulled down her pants as she lowered the head of the bed. Maria soon became distracted when Vanetta began to unfasten her shirt and rubbed her breasts. Vanetta pulled Maria over and popped Maria's breast into her mouth.

I began to work my tongue down Vanetta's side, climbing her pubic mound and diving into her cunt lips. She obliged by slightly raising the middle of the bed, making her clit more accessible. My tongue roamed around her nearly hairless crotch. Her lips were puffy and soft, folding in rhythmic patterns. My tongue climbed the successive lip ripples down into the well.

She was wet, very wet. As soon as my tongue reached her lips, my chin was bathed in her juice. She tasted sweet. I'd found a hidden waterfall, deep in the mountains.

Her clit liked to hide. First darting left, then right, drawing me into the chase. Soon it enlarged, and, hiding, became more difficult. I licked, searched, and sucked from the well.

Vanetta savored Maria's pear shaped breast in her mouth. The dark brown areola was now small, tight. Maria's hand roamed over Vanetta's face, skimming her breasts, pulling on her belly. Gently, Maria pulled her breast away, quickly replacing it with her mouth. Their tongues began dancing.

☆   ☆   ☆

I felt Vanetta's passion rising. She reached her hand down to stroke my head, tilting her cunt. I moved my hand up her leg and stroked her warm, wet opening. One finger slipped in. It was lost in the great expanse. I swam two fingers in, reaching the walls.

She started to grind into my hand. My tongue grew more demanding. I added a third finger. Twisting, Vanetta moaned, from her cunt up through her throat.

Maria held her shoulders and dived deeply into her neck. I could barely hold on. I pushed my mouth deeper into her cunt. Her bucking matched my thrusting rhythm.

Soon we three were dancing across the sheets. As I touched a wet finger to Vanetta's ass, she exploded.

She moaned.

She squealed.

She rocked.

She screamed.

She flooded.

She sighed.

She whimpered.

She rested.

I moved up from between Vanetta's legs to lie by her side and hold her. She rolled over to face me, tit to tit, cheek to cheek. She fell into a soft sleep.

Maria quietly rose, still half-dressed. She pulled on her shirt and whispered, "Bye, kid. Thanks for the adventure."

Slowly Vanetta roused. She touched my back, tickled my ass and moved her hands up to my breasts. She sucked my breast into her mouth and began a gentle tongue washing. She pulled me up to my knees and began to stroke my clit, holding my ass, pulling me deeper into her mouth.

I was hot, so hot. I could barely hold myself. But I wanted my first orgasm with her to unfold when she was inside me. So even though my chest was flushed a bright red, I kept my breathing even.

Climbing off her face, I reached over and dragged my hand across her belly and lazily fingered her cunt lips. Her moisture had come outside. Even her pubic hair was wet.

I couldn't hold back much longer. I rose up and moved my head towards her crotch, my ass in the air next to her shoulders. She raised the head of the bed and began to finger my cunt.

I was hot. I was hot for her touch. Her long fingers played their tune across my clit's hood. Soon they were insisting entrance into my cunt.

She slid in. Her long fingers began rubbing my cervix. She pushed into me. I buried my face in her warm wetness.

I pulled my cunt back to meet her thrust. I pushed my face further into her clit. Cunt . . . clit . . . cunt . . . clit. The back and forth rhythm built. She wet her thumb and rolled it around my clit.

My breathing stopped, my feet curled, my cunt tightened. Then I released.

My waterfall cascaded down her fingertips, through her fingers and into her hand. She caught my come and brought it to her mouth, licking, savoring.

She grabbed my hand, and pulled me up to her. She lay with her face on my tit, her arm across my pearl, atrophied legs intertwined.

She licked my breast for a while then fell gently asleep. After a while I felt soft tears on my breast. I stroked her hair and held her to me. She cried a while then looked up and said, "Nobody's ever done me this good."

"Crip to crip is a very special experience," I sighed. "It's a magic that few will ever know."

Jonny and Vera

La Verne Gagehabib

Vera fell asleep on Jonny's bed awaiting his arrival. She was dreaming about what it would be like after they were married, and how they would make love together. She crushed Jonny's pillow into her face inhaling his wonderful scent. Sighing she continued dreaming. She saw Jonny, but Jonny had breasts! Jonny had small breasts, and a woman's body. They were making love. Their kisses were deep, long, and electrifying. They were lying naked on Jonny's bed. Vera was on top of Jonny lodged between his/her open legs. She was locked tightly up against Jonny, and pressing herself into Jonny. Jonny was lifting her/his hips up to Vera, meeting her every thrust. They were moaning and enjoying each other's womaness. Vera moaned in her sleep. She could feel a deep passion in her loins, that only a woman could satisfy . . . and Jonny, as a woman in her dream, was doing just that. Vera tried to wake up from this dream and return to reality, because this dream could not be, and could never come true, because Jonny was definitely not a woman.

Finally, reluctantly, Vera woke from her dream. She felt a deep hunger for a woman's body next to hers. She gently touched her breast with one hand, while the other hand found her womaness and its wetness. Smiling to herself she thought of how she would share her dream with Jonny. She knew that Jonny would laugh at her and think her silly, but she would tell him anyway. With other men who had shared her life in the past, she could not share such a dream; but Jonny was different, they could talk about anything. That's why she was laying here naked in Jonny's bed because Jonny would probably just come in and say "hi," make some tea, sit and talk like she was fully dressed. Not like the others, the only two men that she had cared to love. They turned out to be only interested in themselves. Jonny wasn't like this. His only interest was Vera, what Vera wanted . . . what Vera thought. That is except when Vera was like this and wanted Jonny's body. Jonny was the one who said "Lets wait until we are married. I want to do it right."

Smiling Vera drifted off to sleep again. This time Vera dreamed of performing a most needed surgery on one of her patients. As the town doctor, her patients depended on her skill as a surgeon and physician to heal them. If only she could heal the throbbing between her own legs, maybe she could then concentrate on her work. At last the first dream was quickly forgotten.

Later, Jonny stood looking down at the sleeping Vera. She was so beautiful she nearly took Jonny's breath away. The covers were thrown back and Vera's creamy breasts were exposed and screaming for Jonny to kiss them. It was an effort on Jonny's part not to reach down and caress them. Vera turned and all of the covers were pulled off, revealing her complete nakedness. She lay on her back spreading her legs apart and sighing in her sleep. Jonny almost passed out at this sight. The triangle patch of red hair between Vera's legs was redder than the hair on her head, which was spread out all over the pillows. Jonny again resisted the urge to kneel down beside the bed and bury his face in the triangle of curly softness of Vera. Instead, Jonny sat on a chair beside the bed still absorbing the sleeping Vera, and removed his boots, changing into slippers. Jonny closed his eyes tightly and held his head in his hands, trying to control the urge to get into bed with Vera and make love to her. "Why can't I just wake her up and tell her the truth about me?" Jonny fought with himself. "Why can't I tell Vera that I am not the man she thinks that I am, but a woman like she is? A woman who loves her and wants to marry her and live happily ever after, forever as . . . what? Husband? Wife? What? This is crazy."

Jonny stood over the bed again.

"Vera . . . wake up sweetheart." Vera opened her eyes and looked into Jonny's, smiling. What a handsome man he is, Vera thought as she pulled the covers up and around herself. She extended her hand and patted the bed beside her for Jonny to sit next to her.

"Hi honey, sit here." Jonny sat on the bed facing Vera.

"Have you been here long Vera?" Jonny asked, leaning over, kissing Vera's cheek.

"Oh . . . all night I guess," Vera said, noticing the sunshine through the windows behind Jonny. She gently touched Jonny's cheek with her finger tips.

"I'm sorry, love, I had to take my cousin out to Joyce's and then it got late, so I stayed. I would have come back if I had known you were here. I thought you were working until today on something?"

"Oh, I was, Jonny, but Dr. Sara finished it so I could surprise you and come for a visit."

"Well shucks." Jonny fluffed the pillows up behind Vera.

"Would you like some tea and something to eat, Vera?" Jonny asked disengaging his arms from Vera's embrace.

"No, I want you. But yes . . . some tea would be nice . . . maybe later." Vera said pulling Jonny back into her arms.

Jonny squeezed Vera then let her go, jumping up from the bed and walking into the kitchen.

Vera propped herself up on the pillows, watching Jonny with eyes of passion. Jonny made a fire under the tea pot and took cups from the cabinets.

Vera watched Jonny. She admired Jonny's shoulders and how broad they were. She especially liked Jonny's narrow boyish hips flanked by a full round behind. Vera found herself planting kisses all over Jonny's body, concentrating on his behind. She was planting kisses on Jonny's behind when Jonny turned around to get something in the kitchen and Vera's eyes were looking at the front of Jonny's pants and his maleness which stood out against his pants. Vera found no attraction there. I will have to learn how to accept that part of Jonny, she thought. Maybe gradually, maybe not. Oh, well. I thought I could never love a man again, maybe I can't, but I sure love Jonny.

Looking at Jonny reminded Vera that she had something to share with him, but she couldn't think of what it was. For now she would just think about Jonny and loving him. Jonny turned towards Vera, tray in hand and walked to the bed. Now, this is the best part Vera thought. He is so tall and strong, and so handsome, with all of that curly black hair surrounding his face. He is pretty enough to be a woman. Vera wanted Jonny then and there, and in the worst way.

"Ummmmmmmmm." Vera sighed.

"What's that all about?" Jonny asked as he sat the tray on the table next to the bed, handing Vera a steaming cup of tea.

"Not now, love." Vera sat the tea on the table next to her. "Let's talk first," Vera said, moving over for Jonny to sit beside her.

Jonny sat down. Vera took Jonny into her arms and kissed his lips, pulling him close.

Jonny returned the kiss, pulling Vera closer.

"Ummmmmmmmmm . . ." Vera moaned.

Jonny kissed Vera, pulling her closer and stretching out full length on the bed.

I've got to stop this! Jonny was thinking, but was not pulling away. They had reached a point of no return. Jonny kissed Vera's neck and slowly slid kisses down to Vera's breast.

Jonny enclosed Vera's breast in her mouth, sucking gently on the nipple until it was hard. Vera was moaning and pulling Jonny closer. Jonny felt that she had never tasted anything as sweet and soft, ever. She gently touched Vera all over, marveling at the softness of her skin. Her head was spinning, she felt faint.

Vera pulled Jonny up to her mouth kissing her on the lips, eyelids, and neck.

"Oh . . . Jonny . . . take your clothes off . . . I want to feel all of you next to me." Vera pleaded running her hands over Jonny's chest, and sliding her legs up and down Jonny's. She began to unbutton Jonny's shirt.

Jonny continued kissing Vera savoring the sweetness and touching her silky soft body.

Vera had all of the buttons opened on Jonny's shirt and was pulling it off when Jonny rolled Vera on her back, kissing her body and licking her skin. Vera held Jonny's head as Jonny kissed and licked her way down Vera's body. Jonny ended up at Vera's fiery triangle. She stuck her tongue into the wetness there. Vera opened her legs with a deep sigh, welcoming Jonny's tongue inside. Jonny liked the taste of Vera and licked and sucked her softness with joy. She explored all of the folds, holding Vera's clitoris between her lips, rolling it gently around between them. Slowly and methodically Jonny licked into Vera's sweetness. Vera arched her body, moving her hips to meet each thrust of Jonny's tongue. Just when Vera thought she would scream from the pleasure of Jonny's tongue inside her, Jonny slid fingers into Vera while she continued licking her, burying them deep inside, slowly moving them in . . . and out . . . in and out. Vera lost all sense of time and anything else except Jonny loving her. She began to thrust her hips frantically, building towards pleasure she had never known existed before now. Finally Vera screamed her joy. The sound echoed around the room.

"Oh . . . Jonny . . . don't stop . . . ever . . . !"

Jonny increased the movement of her mouth and hand until Vera's hips were lifted off the bed, moving in a frenzy, then she stopped in mid air and then relaxed onto the bed.

Vera pulled Jonny up to lie beside her, kissing her lips, tasting herself on them.

"Oh, Jonny, I love you so much!" Vera said into Jonny's ear as she held her close.

"I love you, too, sweetheart." Jonny whispered back.

They slept.

Hours later Vera opened her eyes and looked at the sleeping Jonny holding her tightly in her arms.

Vera wanted to feel Jonny's maleness inside her now. She wanted to give Jonny pleasure as he had given her. Maybe she could once again gain pleasure from a man in that way. She never had liked it, but this was different. Jonny seemed to want to please her first, saving himself last. She didn't want to wait until they were married, she wanted to please Jonny now. Just as she was about to reach between them and touch Jonny's maleness, Jonny turned over on his side, away from Vera. Pressing her body into Jonny's behind, she nibbled at his neck. Vera whispered into his ear.

"Darling . . . ? Why don't you let me please you, too? We are getting married soon, and I am no virgin, so what are we waiting for?" Vera slid her tongue into Jonny's ear, sending shivers of pleasure down his spine.

"Vera, No!" Jonny said pulling away and sitting up on the side of the bed, fixing his clothes.

Jonny pulled on his boots and turned to look at Vera. "I'll be back. I am going to get us some food at Joyce's. Why don't you get dressed and let's go on a picnic later."

"Why, Jonny Wade . . . you listen to me . . . I . . ."

Jonny was out the door before Vera could say anymore.

"Damn. Damn. Damn!" Vera shouted, pounding her fist into the pillows. "I knew if I waited long enough Jonny would show his true self, just like any other man. Taking over and doing what he wants to do. He is no different than the rest of them." Vera sat fuming.

Excerpted from an unpublished novel.

Their Own Desires

Linn Lane

If you can look intimacy long in its sweet face, then I am a woman who can show you your own desires. Usually it is something quite ordinary. For instance, I'll tell you about an experience on the occasion of my forty-ninth birthday.

I was having a little tea party. All my fare friends were there. The gate to my garden was all lit up. I wrapped my boa constrictor, Ego, around me like a stole. I stood in the brightest spot and began to sway. All the women turned their heads.

The women's eyes, as I danced past, bathed me in lust. Among them were two strangers. This couple didn't look familiar. They didn't even look very California. One of them had red hair. I liked red hair. Around her neck was a brown and yellow silk scarf. I wanted her scarf. I wanted her neck. I wanted her and I wanted her companion whose eyes had gold specs that glittered when she met my gaze.

"Where you all from?" I drawled, emulating the accent of the boonie state I suspected they were from. I think they said Arizona or New Mexico, one of those states that's a few hundred miles and several lifestyles from here. I welcomed them to California and moved on. My attention was diverted by the kissing that was already going on all around me.

Have you ever noticed how much women love to kiss? In that particular room at that particular moment, I did not see one woman who was not kissing another woman. As I looked back at the visiting couple I saw that they too were buried deeply in each other's tongues and teeth, soft and deep, wet, daring kisses, over and over, swaying with the music. They had a perfect rhythm. On the inside of my eyelids I saw them naked. I laid them in each other's garden upon a bed of moss. I put flowers in the red hair, and my hand moved down from there. I wanted them both immediately.

I wanted them both immediately and I didn't want the answers to the treacherous questions referred to generally as getting to know someone.

"Was the red henna or natural?" How long had they been in love?" "What did they do for a living?" "How did they each come out?"

No, the visit I wanted was to a quivering place, with all the information first hand.

> For somewhere,
> Back where the waters parted,
> A spark had already ignited,
> Ignited and Burned,
> Already,
> With me, With them.
> Why was that?
> I wanted to know.
> I wanted to know immediately.

So I wove my way back through the throng. As I returned to them the blonde woman was caressing her friend's ass. The friend leaned encouragingly upon that hand, while no doubt describing in the other's ear, the delicious things she wished that hand might do for her. It all felt very light-hearted so, having not the slightest idea of what was actually being said in their conversation, I interrupted with my invitation.

They were completely shocked but tried to hide it. In awhile, however, they allowed me to lead them . . . well actually, I had them walk in front, so I could admire Joannie's ass (by then I knew their names) as she climbed the staircase. By the time we reached the room, Dana, the other one, had even admitted how thrilled they were to have a room where they could make love and Joannie chimed in, "In such a romantic setting too."

I was thrilled as well, and threw open the window, letting in the night. In the garden below, women dotted my landscaping with various sexual configurations. They were fucking in the flowers and seemed not to need a room.

But Dana and Joannie . . . they weren't ready for love's openness as often practiced within a Temple of Venus. Yet, they were very much in love.

Well, my house is big enough for anything, even that, even total privacy. I gave them every option, that one too. That they didn't take it surprised me in a way. They were so much in love. Well, that was fine with me. I liked being around love. I liked being in love. I liked having any part of love and do still.

They took their passion so seriously. It was rather charming really, though I'd seen much the same many times before. I pulled my

chair closer to the window and looked out disinterestedly at the bloom-
ing flowers below. I knew that Joannie wanted me to stay. I wasn't
sure about Dana. They discussed my level of participation. The moon
was big and full of secrets.

I wanted them to feel more at home so I went over and sat on the
edge of the bed. I said, "Hey look, I know what this is like. Just remember it is you who make the rules now, here, make them as we go.
I will follow them. I'll leave. I'll stay. I'll touch you. I won't touch
you, as you wish. If there's anything you want, either of you, I'll get
it for you. I'll give it to you."

Joannie's eyes were deep inside of mine. She did want something
and I had guessed already what it was. Her eyes were big and bright
as I stepped right through them. The opening inside was large where
I walked, stealthily, carefully, through a cave swollen and pink. There
was sand under my feet and I did not reach out to touch. I walked
further back inside. It was black. It was hot and I did not reach to
touch, anywhere. It was she, she who reached out to me, she who pulled
my fingers down to her breasts, who held them there and cried out,
"NO! DON'T LEAVE! Don't go!" I set back down on the bed beside
her again, holding both her hands as hard as I could. Now she was
ready and spread out more on my satin sheets. I sat very still watching
her lover's fingers enter and leave. More! Deeper! Stronger!

Though many claim not to, most women like this more or less. I
like it more myself, and so did Joannie. Her lover's fingers branched
out, clasping her, opening her more completely. Inside there is a sea
shore, filigreed, breathing, searching for life in all directions. Inside is
a desert too, open, open, land, stretching like Texas for miles. I knew
what it was she would like.

I kept it in my drawer for just such occasions. Actually, I kept
more than one. By now Dana's face was all over Joannie's twat. For a
minute I was afraid she would come before I returned with my object
de arte for her pleasure. I need not have worried. Again both of them
were wondering why I had left them. I laughed knowing that Joannie's
excitement would only increase with this little apprehension charging
the atmosphere. In this instance, I thought how lucky that inhibition
had the power to block orgasm, for I wanted to bring something special to this encounter.

I also wanted to put it inside her myself. I ran my hands over the
etched curves of the dildo as I returned to the bed, trying to catch Dana's
eye first. I hoped she would not be angry. Good. She wasn't. She
smiled at me.

It was an extraordinary trust. "Open her legs," I instructed her softly even though Joannie's legs were already very hospitable. Dana pressed down and out on her lover's thighs until we both saw the red cavern of her vulva all the way up. Gently, I tested the wetness with one finger. I carried that wetness up and smoothed it across her clitoris. Joannie flinched and moaned and started to protest. "Shhh," I brought the same finger to her lips. "Sometimes," I said, "it is better just to be simple, to take what is given to you that gives you pleasure. You do not want to talk about this, at least not now."

She opened herself to me truly then, as I slowly put the dildo inside her, watching the sides of her vulva contract around it, all the way down. Looking into her eyes, the whole time, for a long minute I held her there. I felt the land shift. I felt the volcano rumble. I felt the pulse throb.

Then I took Dana's hand and placed it where mine had been. "This," I said, "is for you, too. In fact it is just for you two, to finish." As I stood, Joannie again reached for my hands, but as I explained earlier, I respect privacy, in a way, both my own and other people's. "I told you," I said, "that I only wanted to watch." And now I was able to, from my chair by the window.

The next morning at breakfast I gave her something, something for both of them really, something that had been mine, that carried a sense of the freedom I'd known in my homeland with it, something in a plain brown wrapper.

I never did get that brown and yellow scarf.

Excerpted from a trilogy of short stories called *A Visit With Queen Califia*.

One Night Stand

Kitty Tsui

Clean sheets. Lee lay naked in the big bed luxuriating in the feel of them. Clean sheets with their particular feel and smell. Clean sheets were one of her favorite things. That and a walk by the sea. Bare feet on warm sand. Ice cold sparkling cider. Chinese roast duck over white rice. Her beloved ten year old vizsla. Anything made of black leather. Kissing soft lips.

It was a Saturday. A day spent doing the usual chores, not altogether unpleasant. She spent a leisurely morning drinking lattes and reading through an accumulation of the week's newspapers. Then she took the dog to the beach. Afternoons were reserved for grocery shopping and doing the laundry. Lee loved planning meals, shopping for food and clean clothes.

After the chores it was still early. Lee lay on the fresh smelling sheets and surveyed her home scene with satisfaction. Everything was clean and dust free. The laundry had been put away. Books were in their place. Even the towels in the bathroom had been folded just so. She smiled and leaned over to pet her dog, stretched out asleep beside her. She liked it when everything was in its place. Orderliness gave her a sense of control.

Lee closed her eyes and began to touch herself. When her nipples began to respond she took them between her thumb and index finger and gave them a sustained pinch. She could feel the juices welling up hot between her legs. She turned onto her stomach, positioning her cunt on top of her hands. Slowly her pelvis started to move. Slowly at first, then faster and faster, her small bare ass moved in a patch of afternoon sun. Soon the silence was broken by her short, sharp cries.

Lee was dozing when MJ came into her mind. Lee had met her in New York a couple of years ago on a trip to meet with a literary agent. On her last night in Manhattan, she had gone to the Duchess, a lesbian bar, to have a drink. She had planned to have one drink and return to the hotel. But that was before she saw MJ.

MJ had been standing at the bar smoking a cigarette and listening with feigned interest to an argument next to her. She was smiling a crooked smile, as if she knew a secret that was hers alone. She was a tall woman, light enough to pass, if her nose and full mouth did not give her away immediately. She followed Lee with her eyes almost from the moment Lee passed her at the bar. Lee hadn't finished half her drink when the woman approached her and said. "I'm MJ and I've never seen you here before."

Lee liked her directness immediately. Later MJ had said, "Don't see too many Asian women here. I love Asian women. I'm one too, you know. My real name's May Jade. My mother used to play mah jong all the time and she'd call me MJ for short. So it kinda stuck. Everyone calls me MJ." She laughed. "And can you see a black Chinese dyke answering to the name May Jade White!"

They laughed and talked easily. Both related to growing up in Chinese households with Lao Yeh and Poa Poa. Both admitted to liking Asian women and, later on, admitted to liking each other. They talked and danced until the bar closed. Lee wanted to spend the night together but asked, instead, if MJ wanted to go for a supper of noodles or jook.

It was five on a cold spring morning when they hailed a cab on Canal Street to take them uptown. Inside, in the warmth, Lee took MJ's face in her hands and kissed her full on the lips. And could not draw herself away. They were soft and warm, surely the softest lips she'd ever kissed.

The cabby drove through the night. City lights, traffic sped by. MJ flirted with Lee, throwing looks from piercing gray eyes. Tickled her earlobes with quick darts of her tongue. Kissed her relentlessly, hard on the lips, with an insistent tongue.

Lee pulled away and said breathlessly, "You're married . . ."

"You're not," came the reply.

"We're in a taxi, a moving vehicle . . ." Lee tried again.

"You think you're the first one in his cab . . ." MJ laughed. "Your next excuse will be that you're a nice Chinese girl."

"I am . . . you are . . . we were . . ." But MJ was unbuttoning Lee's shirt and kissing her exposed skin. "I want you," she whispered. "I want you real bad."

The next thing she knew the taxi had stopped and they were at her hotel. Lee couldn't believe it when MJ had insisted on going home. "I'm expected," was all she said. "I'm already past late. Call me if you're ever out this way again. Or I'll call you." And she was gone.

Lee watched the tail lights of the cab until it turned and was out of her sight. She spent the next few hours pacing in her room until it was time to go to the airport. She was angry and restless and couldn't sleep. She was upset that MJ's flirtation had been just a tease. She was upset that her body had responded, that MJ had fired her so from the wetness between her thighs to the warm tingling in her toes. Lee hated having insomnia, even if it was already dawn. And she hated being rejected on her last night in New York City. Really couldn't even call it a one night stand.

☆   ☆   ☆

The telephone rang, jolting Lee from a deep sleep.

"Is this Lee?" asked a voice she couldn't quite place. "This is MJ. I hope you remember me."

Lee drew in her breath sharply. You've done it again, she thought to herself, you've conjured her up and now she's here.

"I'm in town on my way to L.A. and have a free night. I'm sorry about the way things ended the last time, but I'd like to see you tonight. Is that possible?"

One part of Lee thought — great! There's food in the fridge and the house is clean. I also have a free evening and I'd love to see her. But the demon shouted — fuck her! She rejected me, teased me and dumped me. I don't want to see her again.

"I'd like to see you, too. But I have to tell you I was hurt we didn't get to sleep together."

"I wanted you, too. But I was afraid to come too close to you. That's why I left."

"Come over," Lee said, without any hesitation, "right now."

MJ was dressed in tight black jeans and a white silk shirt. Red Reeboks were on her feet. Lee had been very tense, not knowing what to anticipate from the meeting. But when she opened the door and saw MJ and how she was dressed, she burst out in a loud laugh. "You look more like a Californian than a New Yorker. Look at you!" She could not hide the pleasure in her voice.

"Surprise! I *am* a Californian. I've just been living in New York trying to find a gig while I was taking dance lessons. I may be moving back to California."

Lee drew her close and kissed her without any hesitation. Many minutes passed before Lee realized that they were standing in the doorway and the front door was still open. "Come in." she said, breathlessly. "Want a drink? You hungry or anything?"

"I'm hungry," MJ replied, "I've been thinking about you since the day we rode around Manhattan in the back of the cab. I want you. I want you really bad."

Lee took off MJ's red shoes and white socks, her jeans, shirt and black lace underwear. She kissed her all over her body until she thought she would faint from desire. Lee pinned MJ under her body and, starting at the core, stroked her clitoris, her mouth, her nipples, her neck. MJ held onto Lee's solid, muscular body and opened herself up to her mouth and to her hands. She was wet when Lee's fingers found her opening, and she shuddered when Lee plunged inside her with a power she had never felt before. They moved together, in a rhythm that was strong, deep and steady.

☆ ☆ ☆

MJ came to orgasm in a way she had never experienced before. Lee's hand was inside her, Lee's mouth on her clitoris. All of MJ's awareness was centered on her cunt where Lee's fist moved inside her in a delicious rhythm, generating incredible waves of pleasure. She felt herself tense, peak, open and open, shuddering uncontrollably in the release. MJ expected Lee to stop when she felt her orgasm, so she gasped and cried out when it was apparent that Lee was not finished.

"Keep coming for me, baby. Yes . . . yes, that's right." Lee hissed as she moved and thrust and brought MJ to orgasm after orgasm with each stroke. "Yeah, baby, I know you've been waiting for this. Let me fuck you and fill you and make you feel sooo good."

☆ ☆ ☆

It was way past midnight when passion released them. Lee put on an oversized shirt and went into the kitchen. "Still hungry?" she grinned. "We've got lots of choices here tonight. If you can't wait we can have toast and tea or a bowl of saimen. On second thought," she continued without giving the other woman a chance to get a word in, "I picked up a package of steaks. How'd you like to have steak and eggs. And maybe some fried rice?"

"Darlin', I'll eat anything with you right now," MJ smiled, "anything."

Lee came back to the bed and ran her hand along the length of MJ's body. "If I fix you a great meal, will you come back again?"

"Uh huh. You bet I will, baby."

"You're a beautiful woman," Lee said with great tenderness. "And I love those lips of yours." She bent to kiss her, gathering her up in her arms.

"Oh, baby," MJ moaned, "you're so good. Besides, I never did like them one night stands."

Happy Birthday To Me

L. (Treth) Tretheway

"Happy birthday, dear Maryanne . . . happy birthday to me." Maryanne finished the tune just as she lit the last candle. The heat from the forty candles in front of her made her draw back and check her eyebrows and bangs for singed edges.

She filled her lungs with air, slowly, while voices from her childhood chanted in the background, "Only one breath or your wish won't come true!" She thought for a moment and made her wish. With closed eyes she inhaled deeply then forced the air through her small, rounded mouth and leaned toward the flickering lights, increasing the flow and velocity, making a sweeping motion with her head, going around in a circle, snuffing out each and every one.

She stayed at the table, watching as the red-orange ends of the wicks faded and gave way to thread-like wisps of smoke which rose into the absence of light and disappeared a few feet above her head.

Reluctant to end her celebration, Maryanne sat there, her eyes adjusting to the dimness of the room, playing with the droplets of wax given up by the candles all over the thick, rich, dark chocolate icing. After she had gathered them up and made a tiny pile, she began to suck the candles, one at a time, savoring the gooey frosting clinging to the bottom of each one.

By the time she finished sucking the sweet stickiness from the last candle, her stomach was growling, impatient for more substantial gratification. On her way to the kitchen she turned on the lights.

Forty. How did I get to be forty and not even notice it creeping up on me? The thought hit her at the same time the sudden brightness caused her pupils to contract. She gathered up a napkin, plate, knife and fork from their various assigned places in cupboards and drawers.

Back at the table, she carefully drew the knife down through the moist chocolate in front of her and lifted out a wedge, balancing it on the narrow blade before letting it fall to the plate, scattering crumbs everywhere.

Forty. Forty. The Big Four Ohhhhhhh. Middle age. Her thoughts marched along to the rhythm of her teeth banging together as she chewed. Forty, Forty, Forty, Forty, swallow, forty, forty, forty.

Forty years. A lot had happened to Maryanne in forty years. Her life was like a book she had read quite awhile ago. Not an opened one, but one that was closed tight and gathering dust.

I remember my first birthday and the doll I got. It was as big as she was. It's arms and legs were made of red flannel and it had a hard plastic face which cracked and peeled away over the years until there was nothing left but the edges and the nose stuck in the middle of the missing face. For years, she had thought that was what happened when people got old and wrinkled. Even now she would occasionally examine her face whenever she noticed a new wrinkle and check to make sure her skin was intact.

Forty years. When she thought that far into the future, the years stretched out beyond the limits of her mind's vision, like a highway through the desert, going on into forever.

The preceding forty years, however, were all stacked up, one on top of the other, no memory any nearer or farther away from the present than the next. Like a giant high-rise apartment building. Each year warehoused within a floor of that structure. Each floor full of rooms housing events, moments, experiences, dreams, some realized and some that never came true.

She hadn't thought of time like that before; the past as vertical, the future, linear. *So, after it was all over, at the dying time, you didn't see your life pass before your eyes like a moving picture show. You stood in front of it and looked it up and down.* Maryanne liked that idea and smiled to herself as she cleared her plate from the table.

While the water ran from the tap, rinsing away the last evidence of the birthday cake, Maryanne took inventory. *OK, so I'm middle aged. When I was ten that was incredibly old. But, now . . . hell, most of my friends are middle aged and they're not so old. We're all just kids still. Yeah.* She found comfort in that realization and snapped the towel for emphasis before hanging it back on the refrigerator door handle.

With the rest of the evening stretching before her, she began to wander through her apartment wondering how to make the time go faster. As she passed the telephone in the hallway, she felt pulled towards it. *I know, I'll call Ellen. She'll remember it's my birthday and she'll do something wonderful to make me feel better.*

After letting it ring seven times, she hung up. *Damn! My best friend. Where the hell is she? She's supposed to be there when I need her.*

Maryanne went back into the living room and turned the television on. A scene from "Golden Girls" was in progress. The show was a situation comedy about four older women all living together in a house in Miami. Tonight they were trying to console Blanche, who had just begun menopause. She was upset about the anticipated loss of her sex life. The others were trying to reassure her that her sex life didn't have to be over.

Maryanne turned the television off. I don't need to be reminded about that. At least Blanche has had an active sex life to miss. I can't even remember the last time I. . .

Maryanne twisted sideways on the couch and let her legs stretch out the length of it. With her hands behind her head, she watched her feet help each other off with her shoes and made her toes wiggle, one at a time, like small finger puppets.

She started to think about the last lover she'd had. Her name was Vicki. She was nineteen years younger than Maryanne, and while it didn't seem to bother Vicki, Maryanne had been constantly aware of their age difference. And self-conscious about it.

At first, she was able to respond to Vicki's seemingly endless energy for love making. She was inspired and almost obsessed with it. But, after a few months, Maryanne had begun to be too tired at night or too distracted during the day. She longed for a more relaxed and comfortable sexual relationship. The intensity and passion had been exciting and welcomed at first, but very soon it got to be too much too often.

Her hands snuck out from beneath her head and started moving down the sides of her body now as she remembered the last time they had made love. Fortunately, it was a graceful parting, each realizing that what they needed wasn't going to be found with the other. Besides, Vicki was going back east to school and the chances for successfully maintaining a long distance relationship were slim. They both knew it.

That last night, many months ago, had been special with candles and soft music, cheese fondue and cracked crab. Her hands reached around to rub the small of her back as she recalled the delicate pressure Vicki had applied while giving her one last massage.

Maryanne brought her hands around to her stomach, slipping them under her t-shirt, tracing light circles around and around on each side of her belly button. Through her closed eyes Maryanne could see Vicki straddling her hips, leaning over her, tracing the same circles, her breasts swaying back and forth as her hands moved around and around.

She saw Vicki in her memory-eye lean over her further still and could feel her bring her hands up to rhythmically squeeze and release her breasts. Her own hands followed that path and she took each of her nipples between her fingers, pinching and tweaking them, remembering the pleasure Vicki had given her and feeling the pleasure she was giving herself now.

She became Vicki, imagining the presence of her own nipples in her mouth, against her tongue, between her teeth as she chewed and licked them. She could taste the tangy sweetness of the thin drops of moisture that she coaxed out with her sucking.

She left her breasts and undid the buttons on her jeans, easing them over her butt and off her legs in one fluid motion, kicking them to the floor once they reached her feet. She drew her fingers up the length of her legs feeling with satisfaction their solid strength. Maryanne smiled, remembering the sincere appreciation Vicki had expressed at the muscle tone and definition of her legs the first time she had seen Maryanne naked.

Her journey ended at the tops of her thighs where her fingers became immediately tangled in her pubic hair. She parted her vulva and let the air in to counteract the sensation of heat she had begun to feel between her legs. With her outer lips separated, exposing her clitoris, she used her fingers to explore her opening, looking for moisture. She was not disappointed.

As her fingers slid to the source of her dampness, scooping up the precious wetness and spreading it up and down her slit, she could see Vicki looking up at her, smiling with her eyes as she lapped up the juices with her tongue, two fingers inside, rubbing the top of her secret place.

Maryanne remembered the way Vicki would tease her with her tongue, licking fast and then slow. Applying tremendous pressure and then withdrawing altogether, or, even more maddening, pulling away far enough so that she wasn't sure if Vicki was actually making contact or merely softly blowing on her clit.

Her fingers became Vicki's tongue. She began to rock back and forth, then lift her pelvis slightly, her fingers hanging on for the ride. She could feel her heart beating harder and faster in her chest. Her neck throbbed with the pulsing of blood rushing up and down her body, hurrying to flood her clitoris which was swelling now under the deft manipulation of her hand.

Beads of perspiration appeared on her forehead and began to meander down the sides of her face. She could hear Vicki moaning with feral sounds deep in her throat and realized it was she herself who was making love music. She felt as much as heard the groans rumble in her chest as her throat and vaginal muscles tensed in unison. She was beginning to come.

Her orgasm built within her as Maryanne watched Vicki leave her mound and sit up to thrust more deeply into her with her fingers. She touched herself on the outside while she squeezed her vaginal walls around the two fingers she remembered inside of her. She rubbed herself faster and faster, moving her hips up and down to make the most of the imaginary fingers stroking her insides.

All the muscles in her body constricted at the same time. Her toes curled. Her buttocks tightened. Her legs straightened, stretching beyond the end of the couch. All sensation began to rush to the center of her abdomen. Like a sneeze on the verge of exploding, her entire body prepared for the final contraction which would precede her climax.

She lifted her shoulders, curling up in a sitting position, her knees drawing up, her fingers still vibrating her clit. She could see Vicki licking her own bow-shaped lips in pleasure, her hand moving in and out. Maryanne could no longer stand it.

With one last great shudder, her orgasm arrived. Like a single drop of water falling into a pool, it rippled out from her center, wave upon wave washing over her. Her body rocked with the waves like a small boat in the aftermath of a storm.

It passed. She relaxed into a puddle of soft flesh and brought her fingers to her mouth, licking them clean, tasting herself, smelling the sweet musty smell lingering there.

She sighed. A heavy, satisfied sigh.

"Happy birthday, dear Maryanne . . . Happy birthday to me," she hummed as she drifted off to sleep. *Forty, forty, forty. Hmmmmm, not bad.*

The Medicine Song of Allie Hawker

Paula Gunn Allen

It was a soft and female night. The air of the high plateau's desert was silky and balmy, skin caressing, lung-loving. High in the rocky hills far above the town, Allie and Raven watched the stars fall. The sky was soft and warm. The stars as close as the city lights burning scattered jewel flame on the desert floor below. Soft and warm and sweet. More intoxicating than anything could be, anything at all. Except . . .

Except the feeling of the woman beside her. Except the sweet liquid warmth pulsing through her body and wetting her cunt. There they were, caught between the points of light above and below. Held in the sensuous strokings of the night air. Caressed and stroked, relaxed and throbbing. In time to the throbbings of the stars, of the moving cars on the dark streets far away, below. Allie knew they would make love soon. She didn't want to hurry. She wanted them to melt into the sky stars desert rocks mountain's high peak, each other. She would wait for that. For the exact time when coming together was complete, entire. Would make each of them, all of them — stars, mountains, desert plants, rocks, peaks and surrounding cityfolk, whole.

"Allie." Raven's hand stroked Allie's bare arm. "Allie," she breathed again. "It's so beautiful here. I've never been so content, so held."

"Me too," Allie said, her voice low and husky. "Only on the desert, on certain rare nights, with certain rare people, can we be like this. But rare or not, it's enough. We are blessed, you and I."

Allie Hawker and Eddie Raven had been lovers for a short time. They had met a couple of months before at a gathering on the rez near Seattle. Not that either woman was Salish. Allie was Cheyenne, from Oklahoma a long time before, and Raven was Mississippesh, the last living person of that blood. Allie, in her late thirties, was medium height and stocky.

Physically, she was strong, keeping her muscles rippling by hard physical work and frequent trips to the Washington wilderness where she camped alone for weeks at a time, seeking guidance from the spirit people and animal people. Though she had not been raised in any particularly traditional Cheyenne way, and had spent most of her life away from her home town in rural Oklahoma—first at boarding school, then in the Army during the Second World War—her connection to the spiritual rivers that flowed through the wilderness throughout the continent was powerful and deep. She did go home to stomp dance every chance she got, and kept in touch with Choctaws through the moccasin telegraph and random encounters with those who showed up in Seattle or wherever she might be. She wore her hair long, usually letting it go as it would. Her broad-palmed, strong-fingered hands matched her face.

In the twenty years since the war she had worked at a variety of jobs. Her chance placement in the offices that worked with the earliest computers had made her after-the-service future secure—that, and her inclusion in the tight circle of lesbians her commanding officer had gathered around her. Just before the peace was upon them, Captain Bee, as they all called her, had gotten word that a campaign against women was brewing in the halls of power. It would become a lesbian hunt, of course. She had counseled her "girls," as she called the women under her—figuratively and not-so-figuratively—to get out while the getting was good. Allie had heeded the warning, and Bee, who had lots of contacts because of her social and military position, had helped her secure a job at the University of Washington, where computer technology research and development had continued.

But, after fifteen or so years in the northwest, Allie was readying for a new stage. She had developed and refined her technological expertise along with the burgeoning computer industry. While it would go a lot further, she knew, she also knew she needed to get into some field that would put her in more regular, institutional contact with Indian people. Her spirits told her that times were coming soon when her direct involvement in developing forces would be needed. They had told her Raven was coming.

Actually, a raven had told her that she was sending a relative of hers to Allie, for Allie to teach and to care about. Only a few months later Raven had showed up, and the attraction Allie had felt for her had been the most powerful feeling she had ever known. She had felt it before she knew Raven's name, or even her gender. Before she could clearly see Raven's face, a face become so dear in such a short time.

They had come to Tucson together so Allie could investigate a guidance counseling program offered at the University there. And for other reasons, reasons as precious to Allie as Raven had become, but which had been a part of her life for a much longer time. It was time to leave the northwest. Her meeting Raven had told her that. She had wondered for some time why she hadn't left, returned home, or to home country, or gone somewhere. She had stayed in Seattle because that was where she had mustered out, because she had a good job, because she had a lot of growing to do, because it was where she was, where she found herself. But still, she often wondered why she wasn't someplace else — Nevada, say, where so much of her true work was — or New Mexico.

Tucson didn't seem like it was close enough to either for her purposes, but she had been drawn there by some force she didn't question. She went where her feet (or was it her nose?) led her, and that had been here.

Eddie Raven, twenty some years younger than her companion, had been raised in the northern regions, around Lake Michigan and Lake Superior. The only child of people who had died in her infancy, she had been raised by her great-uncle, her mother's uncle, the last, but for her, living member of their tribe. He had taught her all he knew, taking her far into wilderness areas, taking her to Turtle Mountain, to Canada, to the northern tundra. She could talk the language, though there was now no one to talk with, and she could engage in enough ritual practices to keep the sacred tradition alive, at least as long as she herself survived. In her twenties, she was a graduate of Northwestern University, well-heeled, handsome in her tall, slender elegance, self-assured and filled with life. And young! So young. Allie's heart filled with tenderness. A yearning over this woman-child, her lover and companion. And more, her friend.

She loved Raven. How she loved her! She was hungry for her, always hungry for her it seemed. "Sure you're not Chinese?" she said, putting her arm around Raven and drawing her close.

"Huh?"

"Seems like I no sooner eat you than I'm hungry again!"

"Alice Hawker!" Raven exclaimed, delighted with her joke. "No, I'm not Chinese. But I had some ancestors who went to China long ago — thousands of years ago. They became the Mongols."

"Well then, they went to Mongolia, right?"

"Mongolia, China, what's the difference between cousins?" Raven said, her throaty voice sending a delightful tremor through Allie's breasts and belly, culminating deliciously in her clitoris. It began to throb in time to the throb of the stars, of Raven's voice, of the silent carlights flickering sweetly in the distance below.

Raven began to nibble Allie's neck, holding her hair away from it with one hand, caressing her throat and shoulder beneath her shirt with the other. "But don't tell the white folks. They like to think the Chinese-Mongolians came here so they can believe we're all immigrants."

"Yeah, nobody here but us aliens," Allie murmured, barely able to remember words as she sank more deeply into the sweet cave of their passion. She could see Raven's eyes gleaming in the starlight. She could see, just beyond Raven's dark head, the stars. She closed her eyes, then opened them for a second, during which she saw an explosion of falling stars. Or thought she did. Maybe it was her own self, exploding deep inside, for Raven had put her long, strong fingers around Allie's breast. She had found Allie's nipple, had begun to stroke and pull it gently. "I'm dying," Allie whispered. "Probably I already died."

"And went to the happy hunting grounds," Raven murmured. She was intent on undoing the snaps on Allie's western shirt with one hand. She gave up and used both hands, unsnapping it quickly, gazing steadily at Allie the while, and opened it, exposing Allie's breasts to the starlight, to the soft, sultry night. Then slowly she lowered her head and fastened her lips on one nipple, taking the other delicately between her fingers. She began to suck, to squeeze. Carefully, slowly. Taking all the time in eternity. Giving as she took. Powerfully, sweetly, deeply sunk in the smell of her beloved, in the nearness of her skin, its smooth stain, its soft gleam in the light of the stars.

Allie touched Raven's hair softly, filled with awe as powerful as the passion that coursed through her in a rising tide. She touched Raven's forehead, brushing back the raven-black hair that had fallen forward as her lover bent her head to her breast. Raven's soft breath only heightened the feel of the air on her skin, echoing it, amplifying it. The air and Raven's breath were one, were pulling her into the night, into Raven's soul, her life, her reality. Allie sighed once, then gave in. She was no longer Allie, herself. She and Raven were someone else—not Raven, not Allie. They were the soft night, the mountain peak, the desert air, the rocks that lay beneath them, holding them in a powerful embrace.

She could hear the cicadas singing. The frogs, singing their short lives out on this night, so soon after an early rain, their passion and longing, their lovesong. Hers too, she knew, somewhere in the mind of who they had become. Her song, and the song of the mothers, the old ones, the Old one Herself. We are here in her. We are not we, but her. All of us, loving and breathing this night, she thought as Raven lifted her head and drew away, staring at her with wide eyes, utterly still in her absolute composure. The tiny beads of sweat that sat upon her upper lip and fine, wide brow glittered in the dim light. The mountain raised up behind them, a black lover towering into the deep satin night.

"There's Sputnik," she said.

"Where?" Raven stopped undressing to look at the starwashed sky. "Where?"

Allie pointed toward the horizon. "Right there, see?"

"Oh, yes. There it is. I see."

They sat silent and still until the round point of light dropped below the horizon. Then they both undressed, dropping their clothes into a tangled heap on a nearby stone. "Be careful," Allie cautioned. "Don't drop them over the edge."

And then they were warm in each other. Bodies pressed close along their full length. Close to the smooth satin-sheened rock beneath them, cool and welcoming. Dew forming between each woman's thighs. Hot liquid sweating from hot cave walls. Soft satin walls. Hot to fingers that moved, searching between swollen parted lips, above and below. Eyes shut and open wide. Clitorises raising their veils to reach out to starlight, balmy silken air. Thighs parting. Legs tangling like smooth branches of great towering trees.

Blessed indeed, these two, become rock and sky; lights and soft, throbbing darkness; satin turning to velvet, touched, probed, parted, entered again and again. Nipples taut and rock-hardened peaks. Smooth, cool hands stroking backs and thighs, shoulders and breasts, faces and hair. Eyes lit by starlight, rocklight, high above the desert floor. Blending, merging, becoming the sky, dusted with brilliance, the stars.

Aunt Sarah

Pearl Time'sChild

. . . Certainly it started with the silky blue pajamas. Jo had found them in her mending bag. They were shimmery, and nice to touch, and nice to touch her body through. It put me in mind of my mother, and other women one has seen in such attire.

"We could pretend," I said, mostly joking, "we could pretend that I am a young girl and you are a grownup woman." She looked long into the fire, sending in her streams of smoke from time to time. My mind had long since left the topic when she said, "I could be your Aunt Sarah. You could be Jeannie, home sick with a fever. You're mostly better now, but you still have to stay in bed, and you're bored. Your folks have gone for the weekend, and I'm taking care of you." She glanced up at me briefly, smiled. "Or we could do something else entirely."

Well, we decided to do it. At first I didn't think I could. I'd been feeling uncentered all evening; if I couldn't even manage to be Pearl, how could I be somebody else? But it turned out it was just what I needed. We'd both been tired, and yet it went on the whole night.

Aunt Sarah had made up a bed in front of the fire, since Jeannie was so bored off in her room. She gave her a back massage, teaching her about "bonewalking," walking with one's fingers along the bones of the back, "bonewalking," the sweet bedtime ritual *her* mother had done with her.

Sarah's taking off her clothes for her turn at a back massage prompted a discussion of nudity. "It's one of the things your mother and I don't agree about. . . . Where *I* live, women, and girls, too, don't worry about it. They take saunas together and go swimming and things, all without any clothes on. They don't care if other women see their bodies. I think bodies are beautiful," she said, "and there's nothing wrong with seeing them."

"That's what I think, too," said Jeannie, not for the last time, learning fast.

. . . If only you could know what a sweetly wandering progression it was, how natural and open and innocent.

In this special night, and with no clothes on because of the fever, it was only natural that Jeannie should offer some confidences about "cunny-walking." And that Aunt Sarah should return such positive, loving energy. . . . That some anatomical questions should eventually be asked, and that Jeannie should get to see what a grownup cunny looks like.

Opening and opening. Secrecy is sworn, "cross my heart and hope to die, if I tell a lie." Its limits are carefully delineated. "If I had a friend, could I ever tell her, someday?"

"Well, if you have a good friend, and you eventually do cunny-walking together sometime, then I'm sure it would be OK to tell her. Because then she would be one of us!"

We are both actors and audience, laughing in appreciation at our lovingness, our inventiveness, our dearness, laughing in delight, and then diving back into the story as easily as dolphins breasting. Or is it "breaching"?

It is hard to tell this story. I am afraid of some hearers. We lesbians, living in a world of such oppression and misunderstanding, need to be able to say that those fears of sexuality between gay women and children are groundless. And certainly the numbers of lesbian mothers, lesbian teachers, lesbian nurturers, outweigh the possible occasional case of sex involving children in a ratio of astounding purity compared to what we are learning about heterosexual males. And right now I have to be on my high horse about this, because we would not survive if it were not so. Most of us would never take the risks for the children that actual sexual opening with them would involve . . .

Still, in our hearts we know that in a loving land it could be otherwise.

And here, here was the freedom to create that happening, without fears, because we were "only pretending." Actually, we were two very much adults, very consenting to enact a healing.

☆　☆　☆

As the night evolved, looking became touching, feeling, exploring. "Oh, there's . . . It's like a room inside you here . . . a soft room."

"Your little hand feels so wonderful!"

Such lovingness. Passing on the secret of "the best place."

Seeing Jo give me love as she gives it to a child, the ways of talking, the way she smiles at me, as a grownup treasuring a child. "You always were my favorite," she said. Seeing how we nurture children, doing them the honor of giving them our full attention. (A chance which comes easier, perhaps, to the Aunt Sarahs of the world than to full-time mothers saving shreds of themselves.)

How lovely it was to be a child, and to bask naked in the firelight and in the joy of being seen, heard, treasured.

So easily defenseless, so easily opening up to solemnity. "When I get my first period, you know, that summer we could go to the Grand Canyon. We could go down to the bottom and camp there. And when our periods come, then we'll mingle our blood together, and then we'll be blood sisters.

". . . I've read about blood brothers; they cut their fingers and mix their blood and then they are blood brothers forever. They have to cut themselves. But blood sisters, this is the way we do it. . . . In fact, I'll bet blood sisters were first; in the beginning, I'll bet it was blood sisters."

Sarah's smile was so soft into the firelight. "What made you think of the Grand Canyon?"

"I was there once with Mom and Dad. And, you know, I kept thinking how it seemed like a gigantic cunny. Of course, I didn't say it to anybody, but to me it seemed like a great Cunny of the Earth."

Well, Jeannie kissed Sarah's cunny and explored it with her tongue and lips. And Sarah showed Jeannie what an orgasm was by having one, and Jeannie, lying on her tummy, felt it in herself from Sarah's coming.

They would take some trips together, they planned. They would write. "I'll send you a letter and it will say: Dear Aunt Sarah, Do you remember our Secret still? Love, Jeannie."

"And I'll write back: Yes! I do remember! *And* about the Grand Canyon!"

Sarah cradled the head with its fine hair in her lap. "You know," she said, caught up in the spirit of young solemnity, "We could have lockets . . . with little pictures of us inside."

"Yes! And the pictures, they could be of our two cunnys, yours and mine." Of course, in that case they would have to be very secret, Pearl worried. "Well, maybe they could open with a secret little button so no one would know."

"Good idea!" Aunt Sarah smiled Jo's smile for having an amusing thought. "And the button, we can put it right in the best place."

And towards the end Sarah stroked and explored her young love's cunny, exclaiming over its soft and simple lines, and with the lovingest of kisses taught her gently of the pleasure of her loins.

Pearl got just too turned on to ever find release. So much was unleashed, so much need and intensity, that no answering sensation was ever enough to be enough. But she was full of the feelings of longing for a long, long time, and then in time, without a coming, sexuality ebbed naturally away. The girl was opened in any case, to trust and to such a being in love. And Aunt Sarah, too.

I remember Jeannie declaring, "This is the happiest day of my whole life!" and must smile again at the reckless reckoning of the young.

. . .As the sky began to lighten, they curled together and fell asleep.

☆　☆　☆

When we woke in the morning, I couldn't remember much of my dream. Only this I knew quite clearly: it had really been Jeannie's dream:

Aunt Sarah and I were living together in a sunny house. And at the moment we were installing a power machine beneath the floor. It was an elegant machine: gleaming, cone-shaped, simple, and complex. A wonderful new power machine.

Carefully, respectfully, we were cradling it down into place.

———

Excerpted from the journal *Home, Oh, Sexuality*, an unpublished manuscript.

Dreams of Sapphira

SDiane Bogus

I

In a womonly forest of a feminine land afar, (or near), long ago, (or now), there lived/lives the incarnation of our fantasies, the ethereal Lela.

Lela, the slender, the tan, (or ivory, henna, amarillo) of flaxen hair (or black, red, brown), womon of magic and power, near-goddess, mortal Lela. Once a swan, once a sea, born now the persona of lesbian dreams. She lived/lives for you.

About the provinces of this land are told tales of Lela. Some say she is spirit; some say she is saint; some think she is angel, or witch, or even a myth of eons of womon feelings. But in all such thinking, she is revered.

Candles are lit to her existence. Stars are granulated for sacrifice. Weeks are bathed in holy-love-making, and many womyn who would become lover and second self unto Lela aspire, through the perfumed herb and ceramic creations, to induce her inhalation, produce the statuesque representation that will bring her to life, into the life of so desirous a one.

Lela dwelled/dwells alone. Her cottage is a mirage of wish and wonder, an elusive monument, like love, stilled and languished in by the will to have it so. Mornings find her mistress-bathing, body unclad and sunsmitten upon the soft earth, hands washing away the night's deprivation. Hands, her hands, sliding mathematically and moistfully the length of her self and sex, seeking to determine the breadth of need in all womyn, bringing to life in her daily self the desire that thuds within you now as these words make such feelings known.

Afternoon is not ritual. There is work. There are greens to be manufactured for the pines and palms, plants and upgrowth. There are brooks to be set into motion. There are birds to be sent throughout the provinces to sing the promise of Conjunction.

Such work Lela does as air and swan, idea and inference.

Night ends the day's fast. Food is created. From the bark of the day's trees, stamina and ceaseless age are ingested as tea. From their leaves, and the moss of once stagnant ponds, is a life-salad tossed. From the feathers of such birds as were touched, come the nutrients of her heart's song. Ground, these piney stems are sprinkled over leaf and moss, and give, continually, flight to Lela's longing for conjunction, to our dreams of such tales as these.

II

The village of Sapphira exists as a province of the feminine land from which this tale arises. It was built of will and wish, of soul and sticks, by womyn who were at first few, separatist sisters who had sought survival without men. Sisters who brought with them daughters and friends, cousins and aunts, such relations of love as love allows. And in time, as time is known to widen canyons, the few born of men were many grown of themselves and word spread of the commune of Sapphira, of the communion in Sapphira, of the possibility of Sapphira, and womyn of worlds and lives we know and cannot yet know were drawn to the high ground of amazon survival.

A circular mix of half-moon shaped huts spread over an expanse of land like large brown Brazil nuts, Sapphira existed in a perpetual state of celebration. And without celebration, as we know in our hearts, it had no existence at all.

The huts housed work and love bevies. Two to five womyn often lived and loved under these thatched roofs. As work for one bevy, there was the maintenance of fields of flowers. Flowers were necessary for ceremony, gifts, and inner-hut beauty. Thus the flower bevy served to plant, water, and pluck many varieties of blooms. Their work was done as an event of the pre-sun day. Sometimes, sleeping bevies, not yet required by schedule to rise, were awakened by the laughter and song of the flower bevy as they made faggots of sun flowers for the dawn's meditations/inhalations. Such songs as escape recall when one awakes from a dream are the songs they sang. By sunrise, a member of each remaining bevy would meet the returning womyn with smiles and kisses and receive the various bunches for the day's needs. Such continual celebration!

In the center of the village was a place of fire. A fire-making bevy was responsible for the fresh wood and required lightings of meal or ceremonial fires. Mid-mornings, if one were idle or silent, they could be heard in the womb of the forest calling down from the tops of trees as their garrotes toppled pruned branches. Near music, and with much innuendo, their "laying one down!" would be absorbed by each womon's sensitivity, as well as the barks of the thick trees surrounding their work. And sometimes, innuendo and the need of rest, and the moist gleam of their own lusty bodies made passion, like an occasional fox, spring red and fire-eyed between them.

The moans and pleasure of the fire bevy was celebration, too. It was the expression of the joy and appreciation for their state of being — existence in the continual presence of their own kind. It was passion as celebration. Each knew as the liquid of her loins flowed onto and into the earth, she was giving womonwater to the reaching roots of the trees that warmed them, and surrounded them in the moment.

Such activities of pleasure and survival were the daily order of life in Sapphira. Anything that was needed was supplied by a bevy. Anything that was wanted beyond that was supplied by a bevy member's arms, or the arms of several bevy members.

In the village of Sapphira womyn existed like the 'amazons they thought themselves to be; they existed as you imagine they could.

III

The village of Sapphira was the home of Sasha, the strong, the muscular, the bare-breasted, wiry-haired, ruddy-skinned, arrow-bearer of its province.

Sasha, daughter, cousin, relative of none, one left at the edge of the forest as donation to Sapphira; one brought as a baby to the only world we'd want her to grow up in. And as if her singular induction to the commune of Sapphira had been known to her from baby-day-one, Sasha lived celibate and strengthful. The bevy did not attract her. The touches and kisses of the diurnal celebrations were, to her, banal. And, as not many womyn thought meat eating the womyn's way of health, Sasha had made herself the supplier of such abundant meats as the forest offered to womyn who came to Sapphira with such a carnal addiction.

With the assistance of the building bevy, she constructed a hut for herself. Herein, the rabbits and squirrels of her arrow's sure flight could be readied. Sasha was not ostracized for this, though she felt there was little appreciation for her work among the womyn. And while they did acknowledge her noble undertaking, the womyn would never have petitioned for the task. For who indeed would ever relish the killing of little natures, the letting of their life-blood, the taking of their skins, the burning of their flesh for womon ingestion?

In the forest of her lone days, when her hunt, which was never tainted by cruelty or exorbitance, was complete, Sasha sat listening to the bird's highest notes: the coo of wild pigeons, the caw of scavenger

crows, the twiddly-whirp of sparrows and their calls, like the sugges-
tive jargon of the fire-bevy, excited Sasha to passion that she understood only as a need to be one with the birds. Yet, no language passed
between them.

Though full of longing—an appetite that celibacy could not ful-
fill, Sasha would not have wanted conversation with the birds, nothing
as profane as that. She would have had them bear her up, by beak or
claw, bear her up high, and by empathy beyond that written on the
wind, beyond knowledge penned in books, the birds would have made
her know how to fly, and fly she would.

In the village she would no longer have the need to live as recluse
and killer. She would become the Lela of the legends told around the
night fires. She would have herself be a living womon of magic, of ce-
lestial power, a she who could *bring* the stars for granulation instead
of waiting for them to fall. How Sasha dreamed, and her face never
gave bevy nor womon a sign.

<h1 style="text-align:center">IV</h1>

On the supreme day of ritual in Sapphira, there came to the village a new womon. She was bruised and tattered, a dirty, emaciated,
clearly mistreated femayle, one from, perhaps, a city, a fight, an acci-
dent. And the welcoming bevy, even though reading its postulant for
the high ceremony of Ovum and Atom, took her to their hut, and washed
her, and as they washed her, they kissed her wounds, such scratches
as she had, and they welcomed her and bid her stay, observe, choose
a craft, a bevy, a lover if she so desired. Nourished, made comfortable
upon a pallet, the womon was left to heal and preparations continued
as process and cycle.

The ritual of Ovum and Atom was the means by which the womyn
of Sapphira sought to invoke the presence of Lela, their religious goddess to whom sacrifice was made, candles burned, prayers addressed.
It had long been legend-near-truth that a womon of herbal magic and
angelic powers lived in the forest and in time, a time of her choosing,
she would come and take unto herself a womon to love and share life
with. It, of course, was a myth, a fairy tale mothers had made up to
put their daughters to sleep by. But as daughters grew up and mothers
passed on, the story became embellished with glorious facets and hoped-
for truth. Now it was believed upon.

The ceremony itself was how babies were to be made in Sapphira,
but not every womon was willing, nor selected, to offer her blood or
egg. One from each bevy, as had been discussed among the cohabi-

tants, would be recommended, and if she were premenstrual by hours, or fertile by calendar and feel, she could participate.

The fire of Ovum and Atom was spectacular. Its flames leapt to the heavens in envy of the stars. It sought to singe the bright of the moon, and warm beyond summer's wildest wish.

Around this magnificent fire womyn came one by one to embrace. Some slipping easily into loving, as Sasha did, giving herself two-handed touches to breast and vulva. Others in pairs, threes, fives, interlocked, mouth to body, mouth to mouth, moaning and writhing, as desire would have it. And they had it, their cries of pleasure stopping owls in flight, leaves mid-fall.

Into the center of the circle, just beyond the fire, came naked and salutary, the new woman. Yellow in the light of the fire, she raised her hands above her head, as if to herald the stars, and brought them down over her breasts, sent them to her mons veneris, crossing them one over the other there, she proclaimed, "I am Lela," as if she would be believed.

How could she be? Why would she be? The high ritual of Ovum and Atom had been in futile practice for eons of desire. Why would the dream that nurtured it come true now?

Thus, the womon was ignored by the highly impassioned, those who with fingers or hand deep into the floral opening of a lover were deaf to voice and storm, oblivious to all but conjugation and nova.

Yet, those nearest her, still in the ritual exploration of curve and bone, not astral lost in the regions of kiss, stopped, shocked, blasphemed. For who would dare to speak the name of Lela, now? It was not yet time for the incantation. These stopped and watched the yellows and golds of the fire paint patches of motion on her body. Was this not the womon brought into the welcoming bevy early this day? Was she ill still, come out into the night and festival with imagination awry?

Yet in a gesture without grimace, most like an alchemist's delight, the womon plucked from her pubes a single hair, and tossing it toward the fire, the blaze leapt into a roaring green, shot upward into red, and blazed high and purple.

No womon at the fire could continue tribadal hump were she atop a lover with legs enwrapping her. No womon with eyes closed could have ignored the sizzle of magic in the flames. All unclasped, disembraced, unlocked, unwrapped, stopped now, to witness.

"I am Lela," she said again, her skin green at a moment, the next red, and as often purple to passion's extravagance. "I have come to bless this night with Conjunction. I have come on the moon's one hundredth millennium. It is as I desired and set. Is there one here for Lela, out of difference?"

"Your words are strange," said the eldest woman, coming forth, the cane of cantation declaring her authority. Clutching it like a baton, she stopped at the boundary of the circle formed by the naked lovers.

"For lives and more hope than is in phantasmagoria, we have waited and loved in your name, Blessed Lela. We have pressed vulva to vulva in Ovum and Atom and cried the words of blessing and determination many times . . . many times. Her voice became that of a wistful girl. "I, myself, in the last twenty of my one hundred and twenty years, have invoked your spirit. As a girl and as a young womon, I was postulant many years with the fertile hope of being the she who would bear the child of womon inception. The archives of Sapphira have gone without the name of that child for these many moons. We have grown herbs to feed our passion. We have built beds upon which to lay with you. We have held the hope that your choice would be made for beauty or passion, strength, virtue, devotion, or potential, and you come and ask for one of difference." Her face was a shadow of her former hope now. "Here, Lela, O Goddess, O Wondersaint Womon," she cried, "we are all the same. This province has only womyn of the same belief and touch. Perhaps in the village of Appetence there is such a one. We have only similarity, and are therefore unworthy." She knelt and placed the cane of cantation on the ground, took a step backwards.

"I did not go to Appetence," declared Lela in an anger. "I did not go for all are modelled after myself. As womon of earth and sky, feather and flesh, I am epitome. Do you and they not raise your daughters, instruct your womyn to be as I am? Do you not wish for their lives the song, the light, the freedom, the gentleness of mine? Is this not the guiding doctrine in Sapphira? In the hearts of the loving womyn the provinces around?"

No womon answered for what womon could find voice, believe that the ethereal Lela was here among them?

Had any children been awake there would have been a resounding "Yes!" and "yes," again, for they were so taught.

"There is one. Do you not know her?" Lela searched the faces of the wondering womyn.

"Sasha!" leapt one teen among them, a recent arrival, runaway from the stricture of impetuosity. "Sasha is different!" she declared. "Hey, everybody, isn't Sasha different? Nobody else lives without lover, hunts meat, nobody . . ."

"Sasha," commanded Lela, "come to me, come with me." Her eyes, sure green with recognition, invited Sasha from where she lay.

Jaws set, her ruddy skin made neutral by the fire's red glowing, Sasha stood, her stature strong to hostility, her hands, bevined, hung stiffly at her sides. Her eyes as keen as the screech owl's, as pointed as any of her arrows, peered unmoved by the sight of Lela. "I am not postulant. I am not desirous of you," she pronounced.

Had Sasha drawn an arrow, the womyn could not have been more horrified, shamed, astounded. Yet she stood, refusing to go at Lela's command, or in the name of Ovum and Atom. Stood with her hair a rage upon her head, like a lion's mane starched. The fur bands about her upper arms expanding with her resolution. The ones about her lower legs declaring her force in the wild, her nature as amazon.

Smiling, as if amused, pleased, Lela spoke, "Tonight blood and egg shall build us on!"

Relief, like the sweet sail of orgasm, breezed through the womyn of Sapphira, yet they could not cheer, kiss, nor clap.

In the stun of the moment, before their disbelieving and ecstatic eyes, Sasha and Lela were transposed into the hot green center of the fire, and within a second's birth, they became opaque in its crimson-turned-purple with prospect.

V

"You bring my angry and unwilling body to your bed and life, Lela," said Sasha, a gnarled oak rooted just inside the cottage entrance.

"I bring a womon who wishes to be seared by lightning, and she shall be." Lela busied herself at the effervescent waterfall inside the fireplace. There she saturated a large sea sponge, placed it in a basket. "Will you touch?" she offered it to Sasha who stood like a sculpture before her.

"I will not. I am not hungry for such. I am not honored to be here."

"You, my beloved, are as was this sponge before it was filled: dry, brittle and most unpliant, a state most unnatural to it. But a touch will tell you the truth of your heart."

"I will not touch or be touched. You are the mystic Lela — why do you not wave flocks of wild geese above us to call out this truth of my heart?"

"It is not necessary for me to learn your truth. I know it. It is, my rock woman, that I would have you know I know. But if another millennium must pass before your love will open its legs to my selection, then I can busy myself with waves of many sizes and speeds. I can create surf forever."

"And I will be held prisoner?"

"Have you not always been?"

"Never."

"Always . . . by your dreams. Will you not touch?" Lela offered the sponge again.

Sasha, cautious, curious, intrigued by this talk of all and nothing, reached for the basket, and drew back upon further thought. "Tell me the truth of my heart, and I will touch your sponge."

"And truth you shall have, dearest stone of my satisfaction. You envy my reality, have in days past denied me it. You have hoped to make me become a truth by transforming yourself into what the womyn of the provinces wish. And now you feel cheated by my existence. You are threatened by my arrow of love. You know I will skin you of the hardened flesh, burn your frigidity with my passion. I will do to you as you have the squirrels of your hunt. I am warrior to your being, and you fear the loss of self, the loss of Sasha as separate one and savior."

Animal-wild, pierced to the heart, bleeding with confirmation, Sasha grabbed the wet thing from the basket and flung it against the cottage door. "I touch! You see? I touch! I—I am . . . understood."

The sponge reappeared in the basket, and Lela offered it again. And silently, moved, mouth slightly open, Sasha touched, and softened. As many times as Lela offered, Sasha touched and as such touching is touching, it led to more.

Sponge washed from her onxysmooth forehead to her forested feet, Sasha lay at an angle to Lela's healing bend above her. "I am glad for the red of my flesh," she said.

"And why, strong one?" Lela stroked the face of her chosen, played the music of harps as she did so.

"You would be able to see clearly my desire and shame."

Lela placed a soft kiss upon her lips, "I welcome your desire. And your imagined shame is but the moment before creation. If the potter's clay is to become utensil, she must face the shame of warped tries. No pot is promised, but if attempted with creative hands, with the desire to have a thing of beauty and value come forth, the kiln will fire its perfection in the end." Lela's hands paved a path to the pubis of her beloved, stroked there, stroked hair and formation.

"The village of Appetence has many such womyn as I, why did you not choose there?"

Interpreting, Lela spoke, "Do you mean why did I choose you, sweet Sasha? For the brilliance of your feathers, what else?" Her hand found the point of Sasha's pleasure and pressed it.

"I have no feathers. Why do you tease?"

"I am, am I not?" So Lela knelt to worship at the altar of her amazon, Sasha, the amazon, quieted and docile before her.

Tales such as this do not match the imagination's flight when the tongue of a beloved one strikes the soul's red pearl. Blues in the dark of closed eyes spot and spread. Purples fade and lighten. One's head loses hair and skull. The eyes disappear into the airway and the moisture of the mouth evaporates. Such cries as babies will never make escape the throat and beg for translation. One rises to meet the holy onslaught, and finds meeting desire's thrust half-way is not enough. Failing to possess the moment, control its explosion, its length, she writhes, desperate with loves's driving and pulling, only to be suddenly or easily — one never knows — electrocuted with satisfaction. There remains afterward a sea-that-never-was upon which the body floats.

Sasha's cry at the moment of completion was the hawk's in search of a mate. And, as if fueled by the charcoal of her satisfaction, she pulled the quenched Lela upward by the shoulders, onto her body, brought her mouth within inches of the kiss she'd always longed for, and was frozen by the beatific green of Lela's eyes. Each into each's self and soul, they entered.

"As I have desired," spoke Lela.

"As I have never dreamed," answered Sasha.

The kiss was given, a kiss that like tracks in the forest after a fresh rain, materialized the expectation of inception with Sasha. From its probing, its generation of heat in her feet, feet that had long been soled by earth's mineral leather, Sasha tore away.

"I have never readied for inception. I have never sacrificed or lit candles. I have never believed . . ."

"How could it matter?" soothed Lela. "We are but vehicles of other dreams not within the boundaries of this land. We are the symbols of our nation, but we are not its daughters. They are for whom we are created. *She* is the who we are to create."

"Who will she be? How will she be? What will we call her?"

"She will be the daughter of Sasha and Lela. She will be both maiden and magician, amazon and angel. She will be the conjunction of us. And she will be called Maya, or Patricia, or Judy, Audre, Sharon, or any of the names as the womyn of Sapphira will chose from. Kiss me deep now."

And they kissed such a kiss as brought, in that midnight hour, flower pods from obeisance, and caused the egg of the new phoenix to break open, blessing regions unknown with its peeps and promise.

"It is time," declared Lela.

"No, my womon, I would drink from your fountain. I wish to smell of you, the flower of your wetness. I want to—"

"We have millenniums in which to share and make such love as will freeze the fox in her tracks, make this land but a perpetual spring. We have trees to color and tides to move, and distances to fly."

"You tease me with such talk of flight. I want it so."

Lela's compassion flowed outward to her chosen for she knew that within the moment Sasha would understand all, would have all. "Let us scissor ourselves," she intoned. And they did, these two, one of wish, the other of the wild. And in the night of Ovum and Atom, the satin liquid form Lela's fertile inner place, mingled with the fresh and sudden flow of Sasha's blood.

"For the want of Lela," incanted Sasha, as would have the eldest woman of Sapphira, "in the name of Lela. Let egg and blood build us on!"

"And it shall," confirmed Lela, her lips to the feet of her beloved, as it was with Sasha.

Vulva to vulva, wet to wet, truth to hope, Lela to Sasha gave life to our dreams of Sapphira, and their dreams of us.

A longer version of "Dreams of Sapphira" appeared in *Maenad* magazine in March 1981.

Drawing Out the Pleasure

Tee A. Corinne

Gillian pushed through the door balancing art supplies and a roll of canvas. Smells of sun-warmed wood and ripening fruit gently greeted her. The cottage had a comfortably lived-in look without tipping over the line into messy. She planned on straightening it up a bit before Dora's arrival on Friday. Time permitting, she'd vacuum up the beach sand and bring in fresh flowers. Years ago, when she first started spending summers on the coast, she'd had whole days and weeks to herself, to dream and paint and read. Now her days were often filled with students and the details of managing her career. Dora, her lover of twelve years, had always spent weekdays in the city, first carrying a heavy teaching/research load, more recently with duties as department chair.

Gillian carried the art supplies into the living room and sorted them carefully into place on the shelves beside her easel. It was ironic how her otherwise casual housekeeping became almost obsessive order around her equipment and supplies. There and in the kitchen she wanted to reach out her hand and find implements and utensils ready and waiting for her, surfaces bare and expectant.

She glanced at the large portrait of Dora done in their first year together, Dora in an outrageously revealing bathing suit looking sultry, languid, inviting. It still turned her on just to look at it. The painting had come quickly, in one day, after they'd made love most of the night. Gillian had wakened after only a few hours of sleep knowing she was going to paint it, knowing what it would look like before brush ever touched canvas. She knew the feel that the paint would have going on and the feel of the image that would look back, greeting the viewer with an openness of contact, with simmering lust.

Taking out a cloth, she dusted the simple wooden frame then leaned forward, her lips only an inch or so from the painting, loving all the different images of Dora, held sometimes on paper or canvas, sometimes only in memory. Dora, Dora, she wanted the passion back.

She put the cloth away and unpacked the groceries. Dora had gone to a conference last weekend making this a particularly long separation. In four more days she'd be back bringing the warmth, comfort, and stimulating conversation that Gillian loved. What Gillian wanted, in addition, was the fire, the flame, the hours spent revelling in the flesh which had once been the mainstay of their weekends.

In a slow, languid way she wandered into the small bedroom and stood looking around, as if searching for some misplaced item. It was all so wonderfully familiar, the books piled on both sides of the bed, the woven clothes hamper, the wooden wardrobe closet, the mismatched dressers. Feeling a strong desire to be near Dora, she opened a dresser drawer and touched Dora's turtlenecks and sweaters, so neatly folded, inhaled the camphor and mint and rose sachet.

She smoothed the fabrics, slid the drawer closed and opened another, touching the slips, the old-fashioned brassieres, the cotton panties with their fine lines of lace. She took one of the bras, the plainest, closed the drawer, and carried the bra to her desk where she let it fall in casual folds. She turned on the crane-necked lamp and moved it around, changing the balance of light and shadow. Dissatisfied, she slipped a sheet of dark gray construction paper under the cloth to throw the forms into greater relief. Ahhhhh, yes. Lowering the height of the light for greater drama, she clipped a fresh sheet of pure rag paper to her board, sat and reached for charcoal.

Dora, Dora, she sang, concentrating on the hooks, the seams, the full pockets which cradled and supported those wonderful breasts. Time dissolved in the pleasure of her moving hand, the sympathy between hand and eye, the full fleshiness of the paper with its warm color and pliant, receptive surface.

It was getting dark when she pushed her chair back, stood and stretched. The drawing glowed.

On the following day she taught painting all morning, working among the restless, joking teenagers, the mothers who needed time away from offspring to connect with creativity, with inner vision. Two retired businessmen joined the class this year, searching among the older women for companions, asking Gillian's help with landscapes, enjoying her perceptive sympathy and gentle wit as well.

Today they worked on the dunes and everywhere she looked she saw breasts, rolling, confined in soft cotton, caressed by the breeze. The tufts of grass were pubertal, sprouting from the concave underarms of sand, covering mounded pubes.

She felt her juices run.

Back at the cottage she chose a different bra, nestled it on a pink slip and penciled in the undersketch for a watercolor before fixing lunch. Excitement flowed through her as the forms took shape, letting her know that she was onto something special. She ate with haste, put her cup and dish in the sink and hurried back to work in the colors, seeing the shapes fill out and speak with love. This cloth had held her lover's body and now, in the act of painting, she was also caressing that body through the cloth's memories, through her own memories of the clothing worn, of unfastening and removing the bra, slipping the shoulder straps down, sliding her hands inside and cupping the softness, squeezing the nipples into hard, responsive tips.

With a large, soft brush, she washed in the edges, then stood back looking at the picture, absent-mindedly running her hands over her own body. How had so much time passed? She was starved. The outside light was falling. Her whole body trembled.

In the morning she took panties, arranged them with their crotches toward her, the leg openings looped and spread. She took a hard graphite pencil and worked on smooth-finished illustration board, accenting the curves, detailing the lace, remembering licking and licking, tap, tap, tapping with her tongue; remembering slipping her fingers inside the edges of Dora's panties, through the rough hairs, finding the indentation and following it down, down to the moisture, and then back up to the firmness of the clitoris, and back down, and back up.

She shaded in the folds, the interior spaces, working almost as if she were driven, sitting forward in her chair.

For lunch she combined fruit juice, yogurt, egg, banana, and nuts in the blender and carried a large mug of the mixture back to her drawing table where she sipped it while observing her work through half-closed eyes.

She softened the image with the back of her hand, then darkened and smoothed in the shadows with her thumb and a blending stick. Pulling out a box of pastels, she worked a tint into the paper, accented delicate highlights on the panties, deepening the mysteries. The drawing was very large, imposing, impressive. She remembered the first time she'd looked at Dora's vulva in the morning light after their first night together. Dora's inner lips were small with rippled edges. The outer ones were full, pushing in, hiding their treasure. She had bent to nuzzle there, again, inhaling the moist, faintly salty smell, tasting the liquid like the fruit of the sea. Oh, my Dora, where has that reverence fled? How has comfort overwhelmed lust? What can be done to bring it back?

Gillian decided against drinking the now warm remnants of her lunch, changed into a loose cotton dress, tucked money into her pocket and walked into town thinking about the drawings and about Dora and sex. Certainly familiarity had changed the way they approached each other, but Gillian remembered other things, how she used to plan for sex, make special arrangements for it: candlelight and clean sheets and fragrant baths. She had planned dinners around food that could be eaten with fingers, small morsels that could easily be slipped into each other's mouth.

She had stopped wearing perfume when one of her favorite students developed an allergy to sweet smells. That student had been teaching now for several years, yet Gillian had failed to reinstate the perfume.

Stopping at the general store she found that old scent which had always drawn a warm response from Dora. Would it still? She paid, opened the small bottle and sniffed. The hot flood of memories was instantaneous. Pocketing it, she continued to the wharf-side restaurant where they had dined together, where she seldom ate alone. Tonight was a good time to change her ingrained patterns, the grooves she had polished with pleasure, worn so deep and smooth that she hadn't noticed other pleasures slipping away.

Sitting in the high-backed wooden booth, she ate slowly, remembering the drawings, the excitement, the many different kinds of joy that she and they had known over the years. Finishing with a wine and custard, she folded the heavy cloth napkin, paid, then nestled into the old-fashioned telephone booth with its well-worn seat and wood-framed folding doors.

"Dora, Dora my love, listen," she said, when the connection was finally made. "Listen, darling, I've been having quite a time out here and I'm missing you something fierce and my hormones are raging."

"Yes?" Dora said with what sounded suspiciously like a chuckle.

"Yes. I've been doing drawings of, well, of your underwear, and remembering, um, remembering your body and the ways we used to be with each other. Do you know what I mean?"

"Yes. I certainly do."

"I want you to know you're coming home to a lusty, sex-starved, romantic who can't wait to get her hands on you."

"Forewarned is forearmed. I will bathe before I leave."

"I love you."

"Yes, my treasure. And I, you."

Morning light shimmered through the half-closed drapes. Dora would arrive early this evening. Gillian lay, dreamily touching herself. The two drawings and the watercolor were propped around the room: the final evocative image of panties with their inviting openings, the paired bra and silken slip, the starkly elegant first drawing of a single garment, waiting.

She moved both hands over her body, breasts, hips, belly, buttocks, neck, lips, cunt, thighs. She wanted to know whether an orgasm now would intensify her longing for Dora or diffuse her arousal. She decided to proceed, believing there was a depth to her passion that could not easily be depleted.

Touching herself, she looked at the pictures, remembered the act of drawing which incorporated so much of memory itself. She closed her eyes and pictured Dora, clothed, unclothed, cradling her, touching her, fingering her with that deft and tailored motion guaranteed to vault her over the chasm of reluctance, into the seemingly uncontrolled vibratory shaking that directly preceded climax.

She touched herself, whispering Dora's name, excited by the perfume that would soon, she hoped, excite her lover. The touching had a beauty and form of its own, a forward motion, like the act of drawing itself, like the ongoing growth of loving where the bond is deep.

She came with a shower of sensations, then drifted into the shallows of sleep, the feel of Dora present in the bed beside her, present all around.

She woke to eat and clean the cottage, shower and bring in flowers, then chose another of Dora's brassieres, arranged it on red velvet, brought out pastels and laid in the image on a large, fresh sheet of handmade, woman-made paper.

Contributors

Paula Gunn Allen

Paula Gunn Allen, b. 1939. Professor, Ethnic Studies/Native American Studies, UC Berkeley, 1986–present. She received a Post-doctoral Minorities Scholars Fellowship from the National Research Council-Ford Foundation for research, and was appointed Associate Fellow for Humanities at Stanford University, both in 1984; a Post-doctoral Fellowship from the Institute of American Cultures, UCLA in 1981; and a NEA writer's grant in 1978. A major Native American poet, writer, and scholar, she's published seven volumes of poetry (most recently *Skins and Bones*, West End Press, San Francisco/Albuquerque, 1988), a novel (*The Woman Who Owned the Shadows*, Spinsters Ink, San Francisco, 1983), a collection of her essays, *The Sacred Hoop: Recovering the Feminine in American Indian Traditions* (Boston, Beacon Press, 1986), two anthologies: *Studies in American Indian Literature (NY: The Modern Language Association, 1982)*, and the well received *Spider Woman's Granddaughters, Native American Women's Traditional and Short Stories* (Boston, Beacon Press, 1989). Her prose and poetry appear widely in anthologies, journals and scholarly publications. She lives in the San Francisco Bay Area with her son, Sulieman.

I wrote this "erotic" piece as part of a novel I've been working on for some time. I don't especially write erotica, or not write it, just as I am not especially defined by my sex life, nor complete without it. The women in the piece, Allie Hawker and Eddie Raven are long time lovers. As such, they're bound to get it on from time to time. The offering you read here details a time when they did. I see the land as erotically charged; that is, I think that a deep connection to the land necessarily includes a profoundly sexual relationship with it. In this piece, Allie and Eddie spin between them the essential sexiness of the night, the rocks, the desert and the stars. They do not so much evoke it as give expression to it in their lovemaking. The erotic is not, as far as I'm concerned, anything out of the ordinary or in any way special. It is part of all-that-is, as is every experience of humans and other creatures, whether alive in the white man's sense or not.

Hannah Blue Heron

I was born May 6, 1926, in Denver, Colorado. The name on my birth certificate reads Anna Georgette Benton. To celebrate my embracing of feminism and being an "out lesbian," i took my present name in February of 1977. I attended various public schools in Denver, and went to the Colorado State College of Education (now the University of Northern Colorado) in Greeley, Colorado, receiving my B.A. in 1956. I received an M.A. in Theology from the University of Notre Dame, Notre Dame, Indiana, in 1962. I have been published in *WomanSpirit, Common Lives/Lesbian Lives* and *Maize* magazines and was a contributor in the book *Lesbian Nuns: Breaking Silence*, edited by Nancy Manahan and Rosemary Curb (Naiad Press, 1985).

I like to write about the excitement of sex, and to remind people of the mysticism inherent in it, which i value above all.

Becky Birtha

I was born in Hampton, Virginia on October 11, 1948, into a black family with a high regard for education and literature. My first three years were spent in Virginia and Maryland, but I grew up in Philadelphia, Pennsylvania. I studied writing in many places, from Mrs. Grossman's Creative Writing Class at the Philadelphia High School for Girls, to the Master of Fine Arts in Writing Program at Vermont College. I'm the author of two collections of short stories, *For Nights Like This One: Stories of Loving Women* (Frog in the Well, 1983), and *Lovers' Choice* (The Seal Press, 1987). A collection of my poetry, *The Forbidden Poems*, will be published by the Seal Press in the fall of 1990. A recipient of a Creative Writing Fellowship Grant for 1988 from the National Endowment for the Arts, I usually support myself working part time in the library of a private law firm.

My first effort at writing lesbian erotica appeared in *A Woman's Touch*, a collection which was also a first effort, published by Womanshare Books in 1979. I've watched interest and awareness of the subject grow and change in the lesbian community, all the while trying to remain accepting and supportive of the different ways that passions get played out for different women. I feel we need many options, but sometimes fear that subtlety and simplicity in our images and acts are getting lost among the power plays, graphic details, and sophisticated sex toys. It sometimes seems as if my concept of sexuality isn't even on the map of the current lesbian community. I write the kind of erotica I do to put it on the map, and to keep it there as a loving, affirming alternative.

SDiane Bogus

The author of four books of poetry and a performing artist as well, SDiane Bogus was born in Chicago on January 22, 1946, and grew up in Chicago and Birmingham, Alabama. She received her B.A. from Stillman College in Alabama in 1968, her M.A. from Syracuse in 1969, and her PhD. from Miami University in Oxford, Ohio in 1988. She is listed in *Who's Who Among Women in America* (1983), *Black American Writers Past and Present (1979), Selected Black American, African and Caribbean Authors* (1985), *Encyclo-*

pedia of Short Fiction (1980) *Who's Who Among Black Americans* (1979), and *American Women in the Arts and Social Sciences* (1978). Her books include *Women In The Moon, Her Poems, I'm Off to See the Goddamn Wizard, Alright, Women of Magdalena, Dyke Hands & Sutras Erotic and Lyric* and *Sapphires's Sampler* for which she was nominated for the Pulitzer Prize.

SDiane writes what she does to inform, entertain, shock, titillate and educate the readers of her work.

Chrystos

I was born on Nov. 7, 1946 (dbl. Scorpio, Moon in Aries) in San Francisco to a Menominee father & a mother born of immigrants from Lithuania & from Alsace-Lorrain. I grew up there, went to Catholic grammar school. I've studied with Faye Kicknoway, Kate Millet, Kathleen Fraser & Gloria Anzaldúa. My work appears in many anthologies, including *This Bridge Called My Back, A Gathering of Spirit, Through Indian Eyes, Living the Spirit, Out the Other Side, Gay & Lesbian Poetry of Our Time, Naming the Waves & Art Against Racism.* My greatest influences are the work of other Native writers, particularly Dian Million, Beth Brant, Elizabeth Woody, Barbara Cameron, Joy Harjo & Janice Gould.

I love sex. Many people hate sex. I've been called a lot of names (by other feminists as well as by my mother & school mates), among them whore, slut & sex maniac. In writing about sex, I hope to bring forward the natural joy which is denied by the dominant culture. It seems to me that we must voice our actual sexuality because it has been stolen from us by the mainstream male pornography business, by organized (& *dis*organized) religions & by the governments which continue to forbid our love in many states & throughout the world. It was hard for me to write this piece — to know the line between exploitation & celebration.

Jo Whitehorse Cochran

Jo Whitehorse Cochran (Lakota/Norwegian) was born and raised in the Seattle area, where she still lives. She holds a Master's Degree in Creative Writing from the University of Washington. She is a co-editor of *Gathering Ground: New Writing and Art by Northwest Women of Color, Changing Our Power: An Introduction to Women Studies* and *Bearing Witness/Sobreviviendo*, and has appeared in many anthologies and journals. She currently works for the City of Seattle, Office of Management and Budget. She is working on a novel starring Bob the Cat.

Erotica is a genre I've been writing for years but never published. Most of the erotica is poetry to my lover. The truth is that poetry does not make it into the publishing market as easily as prose, although erotic poetry, I think, is some of the most accessible anyone can read. And my lover and I had to work through the public exposure of what is really a private song and work. So I decided to try prose. Another compelling factor for writing this piece was when I read erotica, it did not seem to be about lesbians I knew. There were not a lot of women of color in body, taste, emotion and thought. There was also not a lot of erotica about lesbians in long-term relationships. I have over a hundred erotic poems written to my lover over a five year relationship. So I wanted to write about the kind of lesbians I knew, about waking up each morning to a spark in the same woman's eye, nothing particularly extraordinary, rather the erotic in our everyday lives.

Corbett

Boston raised me as a 'proper and polite polio poster child' from a large Irish Catholic family. Berkeley stripped away the pretenses and out came a wild, middle-aged, fun-loving, sex-loving, disabled women's activist.

Twelve years of catholic school repression helped make me avidly interested in sexuality. I love to read erotica and have collected many stories from disabled women, some of which I share here.

Tee A. Corinne

I was born at sunrise 11/3/43 in St. Petersburg, Florida, grew up in the South, went North to graduate school (M.F.A. Pratt, 1968), married, moved to San Francisco, divorced, got involved in sex education (San Francisco Sex Information Switchboard, 1974–1978). My work in erotica includes two books of fiction, *Dreams of the Woman Who Loved Sex* and *Lovers; The Cunt Coloring Book* (yes, it really is a coloring book); the graphics for *Yantras of Womanlove* and The Sinister Wisdom poster, assorted note cards, contributions to *Lesbian Love Stories, Erotic by Nature, A Woman's Touch, Sapphic Touch, On Our Backs, Eidos,* and *Yoni.*

I write erotica because I believe sex is one way that we can come to know ourselves and another/others. I think there are truths that one can only reach flesh to flesh, and that loving encounters between consenting adults help create a loving universe in which humankind can grow and flower.

Katherine Davis

I was born in Searcy, Arkansas in 1963, on September 5th. This day is also my mother's birthday, and this particular September 5th was Labor Day. I grew up in Colorado, New Mexico and Hawaii. The last six years of growing have happened here in Eugene, Oregon. Who knows what the next twenty-five years will bring. My education has included college, abandonment, lovers, counseling, and Stephen King and Alice Walker novels.

The first draft of "Expansive Paradise" wasn't explicitly erotic, only full of anticipation and tension. It was published in Women's Press (Eugene,

Oregon) just before I celebrated and prepared to end my first year of celibacy at a Celibacy Party. Shortly after that, it was suggested that I develop the story into the satisfaction that the first draft only hinted at. Fortunately, someone wonderful had entered my life and reminded me of all the things I'd forgotten. Why do I write about passion or sex? Because writing is the only way I know how to appease unrequited or ill fated desires. It's an itch.

Terri de la Peña

Born in Santa Monica on February 20, 1947, I am a fifth-generation Californian Chicana. While I may have gone astray, I have never moved from my hometown by the Pacific. Educated in the local parochial schools and community college, I have learned about life by direct observation and experience. My work has been published in the *Irvine Chicano Literary Prize, 1985–1987, Lesbian Bedtime Stories*, and the expanded edition of *The Coming Out Stories*. In late 1989, two more stories will appear in *The One You Call Sister* and in *Finding Courage*. I am a book reviewer for *The Lesbian News* in Los Angeles. *Margins*, my novel about Chicana lesbians, will be completed in 1989.

Living on the Westside gives me a different perspective from that of Chicanas born and raised in segregated East Los Angeles barrios and rural Southwest pueblitos. The urban Chicanas populating my stories live on the margins of a white-dominated reality and struggle with their bicultural identity. A long-time reader of lesbian fiction, I became impatient with the genre's lack of Chicana/Latina characters and decided to create my own. "La Maya" focuses on one Chicana's finding her cultural and sexual self while exploring the rich history of the Mayan past. This story celebrates the beauty and strength of Mexicanas and the cultural resiliency of their North American hermanas, las Chicanas. While growing up, I never mentioned my emerging sexuality; writing lesbian erotica about chicana characters, I end my silence through the fictional voices de mis compañeras.

Carolyn Gage

Carolyn Gage is a lesbian playwright living in southern Oregon. Born in 1952, she was held as a prisoner of conscience the first eighteen years of her life in Richmond, Virginia. Since her escape, she has chosen to live in Oregon. Gage holds two degrees in theatre and in 1988 won the first Oregon Playwrights Award for her one-woman lesbian show, *The Second Coming of Joan of Arc*. She has begun a lesbian theatre company in southern Oregon and continues to write, produce, and perform.

As an incest survivor, thought is safer than feeling. I have more control over my mind. When I write about sex, I can take the little girl who was raped, and lead her slowly along a predetermined path towards a sexual experience. I can guarantee her there will not be any unpleasant surprises—no sudden fierce expressions in my lover's eyes, no unexpected roughness, no accidental reminders. When I write erotica, I can coax my sexual feelings out of their shell, just a little. And for me, that is a major achievement.

La Verne Gagehabib

I was born July 26, 1945, at 1 a.m., in Houston, Texas. My family lived there until I was eight years of age. We moved to Berkeley, California where I lived until I joined the Women's Army Corps. After almost nine years of military life, I returned to the Bay Area to attend college on the G.I. Bill. I was a strong supporter of the women's movement, and all equal rights causes.

Burned out and tired of fighting for any cause, save for the survival of self and loved ones, I moved to Oregon women's land to heal. I met many dedicated women there who encouraged me in my writing talents. It was in Oregon that my first novel, a western Lesbian story originated. It has taken six years to complete it, in between returning to college and graduating.

I am still concerned with women's issues, lesbian especially, and our place in society. As a womanist, my greatest wish is for all women to come together with an understanding and appreciation of our differences and to accept each other for who we are and build for a stronger future for all women. (Womanist—a black feminist or feminist of color. Also a woman who loves other women, sexually and/or nonsexually—from *In Search of Our Mothers' Gardens* by Alice Walker, Harcourt Brace Javanovich, N.Y. 1983).

I enjoy reading lesbian erotic stories and never grow tired of them. I feel that as a writer of lesbian lives, my novels should include the sexual and erotic portions as well. The lesbian novels I have read that did not include sexuality were like being hungry for a many course meal and being given a toothpick. I applaud lesbian erotica writers everywhere and hope that we continue our craft and proceed on into the visual.

In this story, "Jonny and Vera," I wanted to stress the hardships and challenges many lesbians faced in living their lives back in western times, when to survive as a woman alone, without a man, was almost impossible. Women like Jonny who felt it necessary to pass as men went through many extremes to conceal their identity, regardless of the consequences. There are many parallels between these women's lives and the lives of lesbians today in terms of survival methods around employment, family situations and communicating with each other; in how we maintain our identity and how we strive to fit into society.

Rocky Gámez

I was born on August 16, 1938, in Pharr, Texas. I grew up in the area of the lower Rio Grande Valley and received my education there. I've never taken a writing course nor ever had the desire to do so, because I suffer from intellectual sloth. Some of my stories are in *Cuentos by Latinas* (Kitchen Table Press), *Wayward Girls and Wicked Women* (Penguin Books), *Politics of the Heart* (Firebrand Books), and *Common Bond* (Southern Methodist University Press).

Some people collect stamps, books, sea shells, rocks, coins or whatever genealogy of junk as a hobby. I collect people with all their virtues and quirks and impale them on my imagination. Whenever I need to tell a story, I rife through the haze of my memory until I find the character I need. And although most of my characters are very sexual people, this writer is still very shy about writing on the subject of sex. But somebody has to do it, and since I extract my characters from real life, I cannot deny them their reality whether they be man and woman, man and man, or woman and woman. Whatever the combination may be, their sexuality is theirs and to ignore it or deny it is, in my estimation, character suicide.

Stephanie (C. S.) Henderson

I was born in San Francisco and have lived here all my life. I have a daughter 19 (Lydia) and a son 6 (Bryan). I graduated from Balboa High School in 1969, and attended one semester of New College of California in 1988. The fact that I drank and used drugs is a large part of my story. Today, after 23 years, I am Clean and Sober. I wrote, designed and produced a book of poetry called *Packing . . . and other moves*, and, through a workshop sponsored by the Council of the Arts, I have another small book of poems called *Cutting the Cord*. I am published frequently in *Yoni, A Lesbian Erotic Magazine* and my short story, "Texas '52" has appeared in *Sinister Wisdom*. Today, I am real grateful just to be alive.

Sometimes, I am in the Pain. It is the pain of growth — the pain of caring. It is the pain I have run from all my Life. It comes out in my erotica: Scenarios of hurt quickly are denied as pained Lovers connect and are whisked out of reality.

I write from a place of pain sometimes, reach deep into the chasm of my vulnerability. Once brought forth into the Light, the Place where Pain lives is filled with Love.

Pain and Love exist in the same vessel — from that vessel, my power . . . bleeds.

Willyce Kim

I was born on the island of Oahu in the city of Honolulu in 1946. My birthdate February 18 straddles Aquarius and Pisces. So, watch it! I was educated by Catholic nuns all my life, and one of my deeper more profound fantasies is doing it with one, or with some in a large orgy. When I was not rolling in the hay with my first girl I was busy studying all of English Literature. I have a PhD. in Women's Studies which I earned doing hands-on clinical work in various dorm rooms.

I am a firm believer in the theory that when presenting or writing erotica — less is more. My favorite movie *Entre Nous* embodies this thought. I also feel that the best vehicle for the erotic in literature is poetry, because the writer, through the very disciplined structure of the framework of poetry, can assault or caress the senses without verbal excess. A key element in all of this good stuff is a healthy imagination. As a writer I prefer, in erotic passages, to lead and slowly striptease — always challenging the audience to cross imaginatively over their own private boundaries.

Linn Lane

I was born June 1, 1947 in Bayfield, Colo. when the Moon was in Scorpio, at 3:47 in the morning, with Taurus rising. Since I also had both Venus and Mars in Taurus, any competent Astrologer might have predicted my strong desire to experience and tell stories about sexuality. Unfortunately, no one where I grew up was interested in Astrology, telling stories, or (Is this possible?) sexuality. Naturally, I left as soon as I could and have been providing the communities where I've lived since with things to gossip about. I have a degree from the University of New Mexico and a certain amount of credits towards a higher degree in Communications and Media. Since 1974 when I moved to Tucson I have claimed to be this city's "Only Living Lesbian Playwright." Four full-length and several shorter performance pieces have been produced here. I also wrote, directed, and produced one made-for-TV drama called "Post-Hypnotic Daffodils." From 1983 through 1987 I produced a weekly cable TV show and an International Women's Video Festival for the Tucson Women's Cable Consortium. Since 1985 I have been the Director of WomanKraft, a 15-year-old arts service organization that has a multimedia arts space in the heart of Tucson's Arts District.

Ecstasy is life's greatest blessing and mystery. All my life, I plan to stand for anyone's right to write about it, and I want lesbians to be adequately represented. Sometimes I wonder if I am in the minority among women in my commitment to freedom of personal expression.

While, like my contemporaries, I am often outraged by the trivialization and degradation of women's sexuality in popular culture and in the pornography industry, I'm convinced that censorship is worse for all writers and artists.

Lee Lynch

I was born in 1945 in Manhattan and grew up in Queens. I graduated from the University of Bridgeport in Connecticut in 1967 with a major in English, but learned to write by reading such authors as Carson McCullers, Truman Capote, James Baldwin and Jane Rule. Naiad Press has published six of my books, including *Dusty's Queen of Hearts Diner* and a collection of syndicated columns, *The Amazon Trail*. My most recent book, *Sue Slate, Private Eye* is about a lesbian cat detective.

This story was written to explore the interior erotic life of a middle-aged dyke in a long-term monogamous relationship. The urge to stray, which has controlled Sally the bartender in the past (see "At A Bar IV, White Wine" in *Old Dyke Tales*, Naiad, 1984), remains active. Her mature expression of these impulses becomes the story's resolution.

Ní Aódagaín

I am a white Lesbian Separatist, single mother, editor, writer and small-scale farmer. My daily work focuses on the raising of my six-year-old daughter in a lesbian-separatist perspective; and in the on-going work as community member and volunteer caretaker of Oregon Women's Land (OWL) in So. Oregon, a land purchased to provide wimmin access to land without private ownership. I was born on May 19, 1957, in Fairfax, Va., and was raised in New Orleans, La. I come from an Irish-Catholic lower-middle class background. I studied as a French major at the University of Southwestern La. and at the Universit Paul Valery in Montpellier, France. I received a Bachelor of Science in Rehabilitation Counseling at L.S.U. Medical Center in 1982. I coordinated and was Co-editor of the WeMoon '88, an almanac for wimmin. At present, I am an active member of the So. Oregon Women Writers' Group and Gourmet Eating Society.

As a Lesbian, loving wimmin physically, politically and spiritually is integral to my identity. As an incest survivor, I join the multitude of wimmin who have to struggle daily, feel great pain and overcome many obstacles in order to accomplish these acts of loving. By using words that convey the terror one feels while being sexual (or, for that matter, while thinking about being sexual), an act that is innately one of pleasure, I exorcise some of this horror. By creating sexual imagery, I take another step toward becoming, again, whole; that is, able to celebrate in that which is Lesbian loving.

Margaret Sloan-Hunter

Margaret Sloan-Hunter, May 31, 1947, Chat. Tennessee. Catholic Education, completed 1 year graduate school in Women's Studies, Antioch U., San Francisco, Ca. As a founding editor of *MS* magazine in 1972, I "studied" with Gloria Steinem, who remains the singular most influential person in my life. She showed me how to negotiate, how to articulate oppression and to be heard. In 1972 she said, "I wish you could believe that you, Margaret, are enough." In 1989, I do.

When I came out in 1970, I was somewhat of a "purist" lesbian—smack from the school of "nice dykes don't" . . . use dildos, fuck, penetrate etc., etc., believing erroneously that these things were the property of heterosexuals in their limited sexual activity. With age and experience came honesty, and I committed myself to talk and write about what Lesbian sexuality encompassed. I attempt, in all my writing, to draw images with words, to paint feelings with pen and ink, and to keep it simple, which can be quite profound. In this story I wanted to let people know that "nice dykes" do celebrate their sexuality and get real wet when they dream.

Sabrina Sojourner

Born October 23, 1952 in Camp Lejeune, NC (Scorpio Sun, Libra Rising, and Sagittarius Moon). Family moved to Oakland, California, when she was two. Was always an avid reader but did not get interested in writing until high school when she also became a competitive speaker—Original Oratory and Debate primarily. I owe a lot to Miss Montague and Miss Marty Ainsworth for instilling in me the importance of the written word; Miss Jepsen for aiding me in the development of my speaking voice and style.

I started writing erotica as a way of healing myself, and also to celebrate lesbian sexuality—my sexuality! I am a survivor of incest who has moved into the realm of thriving. Most of the 'erotica' I have read is implicit. I'm bored by repeatedly reading material which merely implies or only hints at what is happening or is about to happen. I wanted to read something that was exciting and celebrating of the sexual as well as the sensual, that combined the two. I discovered that what I needed to do was to write from the inside out, and to find a way to play with words and images to evoke the excitement I feel when "dancing with the fire goddess of passion(!)

Valerie Taylor

Valerie Taylor was born in Aurora, Illinois, in 1913, and grew up in a mostly rural and midwestern atmosphere. She is a peace activist, advocate of sanctuary for refugees, and was a fighter for gay rights before it was respectable, appearing on radio and TV in the fifties.

One of her primary concerns is helping people understand that there is no age limit on sexuality, and that eroticism is natural and healthy, unlike pornography, which involves exploitation (usually of women and gays). She began writing lesbian novels in 1958, partly as a protest against the trash being produced (mainly by male authors), and hopes that the characters in her books are true to life.

Sherry Thomas

I was born in 1948 and grew up in Washington, D.C. Since 1970, I've been involved in many parts of the Women in Print movement: *Country Women* magazine, Old Wives Tales Bookstore, and writing two books on farm women. Currently, I'm a partner in Spinsters/Aunt Lute Books, a lesbian/feminist publishing company.

I wrote this piece in 1975 for the sexuality issue of *Country Women* magazine. I wanted then to write with a graphic honesty about the experience of sex, and to begin to find a language to speak out loud what my body already knew. Though I would write now with less discovery and more wry complexity (four lovers and 14 years later), I still like this piece for its hard edge, its effort to break my own boundaries.

Pearl Time'sChild

When my mother was pregnant they lived with my father's family on "the ranch," which was really an orchard. It was fall; there were all the apples one could eat. Time stretched out long past her due date; the family laughed that an apple a day was keeping the doctor away. I was two weeks late, born October 22, 1940, 15 miles and 49 years from where I live today. Today I have a PhD in philosophy, and a part-time job that has enabled me to return to the town where I grew up. I live on the fringe; the house I built looks out over forested hills, and a mountain, and the stars at night. I live with one foot in academia and one in the very creative lesbian community in my neck of the woods. I publish my lesbian writings under a different name than I use for scholarly articles. I've published in *WomanSpirit, Sinister Wisdom, SageWoman, Teaching Philosophy,* and *A Woman's Touch,* and have written an underground book, *The Auto Biography of Deborah Carr.*

As to why I write erotica, when I do: A) For myself: to make a memorandum so I don't forget the dear and happy touchings that have happened in my life. B) For publishing: Because I cherish "the lesbian imagination in every woman," as the early *Sinister Wisdom,* in sister wisdom, used to say. What do lesbians do? Reader, it's endless, endless. C) This specific piece: Is especially scary to publish. Childhood sexuality is an altogether touchy subject these days. Yesterday, while I was thinking about what a gap there is in our research and knowledge about sexuality, I imagined a book, *The Sex Lives of Children:* what we all did and felt and thought about in our early years. I don't think it would get me tenure, though.

Linda Tretheway

I was born in Oregon City, Oregon on August 14, 1948, at 1:21 p.m. in a red brick hospital that is now an old people's home. At the tender age of 6 weeks, I was brought to Los Angeles by my parents, who, without consulting me, decided that a big city was the perfect place to raise a family. I made my escape 27 years later and have lived in Sacramento ever since. In spite of receiving my K–12 education in the LA City School System, I managed to complete a degree in Linguistics and go on to work in the computer industry. The only reason I work outside my home for a living is in order to support my writing habit. I have written numerous articles for several Sacramento newspapers and had a "tanka" poem published when I was fourteen years old. "Happy Birthday to Me" is my first short story to be printed. Another erotic story, "The Bet" is soon to be printed in Judith Barrington's anthology of writers on *Lesbian Sexuality*. A full length play, *Anniversary* (co-authored with my mother, Cay Tretheway) was produced in 1986.

I write erotica for fun. My personality tends to lean toward the more serious, and I find that I most easily give myself permission to "play" around sex. I wrote "Happy Birthday to Me" as a birthday present to myself last summer when I turned 40 years old and became concerned that, even though I was an attractive middle-aged woman of means, I might now start to "dry up." My partner assures me this isn't so, but I worried about it, just the same. I found writing the story a comfort.

Kitty Tsui

Kitty Tsui was born at 11:10 am on September 4, 1952 in Hong Kong. She grew up in Hong Kong and England, and immigrated to San Francisco in 1968, where she still resides. Tsui is the author of *The Words Of A Woman Who Breathes Fire* (Spinsters, Ink, 1983). Her work, both poetry and prose, has been widely anthologized, most recently in *Gay and Lesbian Poetry In Our Time* (St. Martin's Press, 1988) and *Ear to the Ground, An Anthology of Contemporary American Poetry* (University of Georgia Press, 1989). Her body (and a poem!) appeared in the summer 1988 issue of *On Our Backs*.

In the spring of 1988, English photographer Jill Posener approached me with a proposition to pose in the nude for *On Our Backs*. I confessed that I didn't read the magazine and was frankly shocked by her proposition, but I was also intrigued by it. As a bodybuilder, I was used to showing my muscles, but had never posed nude for the lens. Editor Alison Kim had written a sexy piece entitled *"Who Says We Don't Talk About Sex?"* As another Asian Pacific lesbian, I could identify with her. I posed for the photographs to shatter some stereotypes about Asian women. I write erotic poems and stories so you will know that, yes, we talk about sex. And yes, I hope the talk turns you on!

Tee Corinne: self-portrait.
All photographs by Tee Corinne.

Paula Gunn Allen

Becky Birtha

SDiane Bogus

Chrystos

Jo Whitehorse Cochran

Corbett

Katherine Davis

Terri de la Peña

 Carolyn Gage

La Verne Gagehabib

 Rocky Gámez

Stephanie (C.S.) Henderson

Hannah Blue Heron

Willyce Kim

Linn Lane

Lee Lynch

Ní Aódagaín

Margaret Sloan-Hunter

Sabrina Sojourner

Valerie Taylor

Sherry Thomas

Pearl Time'sChild

L. (Treth) Tretheway

Kitty Tsui